D1612385

ADVENTURE IN THE SKY

By the same author:
Enemy in the Sky (1976)
One Man's War (TV Series) 1963
Where No Angels Dwell (with Roderick Grant) 1969

Adventure in the Sky

Air Vice-Marshal
SANDY JOHNSTONE,
CB, DFC

WILLIAM KIMBER · LONDON

First published in 1978 by
WILLIAM KIMBER AND CO. LIMITED
Godolphin House, 22a Queen Anne's Gate,
London SW1H 9AE

© Sandy Johnstone, 1978
ISBN 0 7183 0166 8

629 · 130924
JOH

Photoset by Specialised Offset Services Limited, Liverpool
and printed and bound in Great Britain by
Redwood Burn Limited, Trowbridge & Esher

Contents

		Page
	Foreword	9
1	The Expensive Lesson	13
2	Picking the Team	20
3	All Fares Please	26
4	Hard Lines	34
5	For Hire and Reward	41
6	Call to the Colours	49
7	The Tail-End Charlies	58
8	Take Cover	64
9	Southward Ho!	71
10	Baptism of Fire	79
11	The Age of Chivalry	86
12	The Defenders	93
13	Unlucky for Some	101
14	A Matter of Urgency	110
15	The Milk Run	119
16	The Dorcheser	126
17	The Staff of Life	134
18	Offensive Capers	143
19	A Single to Blighty	151
20	What Goes Up	159
21	The VIP's	167
22	Web Feet	175
23	Jetting into Trouble	184

List of Illustrations

Facing page

Some hours after crash-landing on the Scottish hillside	32
Abbotsinch in 1934	32
On the promenade at Portobello	33
Hawker Harts of 602 Squadron	33
Shewell's Hart	33
With Corporal Burnett and Spitfire Q	64
HMT *Almanzora*	64
La Maison sur la Dune, Beirut 1941	64
Cannon armed Hurricane at El Bassa with Butch Barton alongside	65
Reconnaissance photograph of small chemical factory at Pochino	65
The Halifax which crashed into the WAAF site at Fairwood Common	128
'Humbug Master' with his 'personalised' Spitfire	128
Lieutenant Helmberger surveys his Liberator – Fairwood Common	128
A Mosquito six	129
Bentley Priory	129
View of Bentley Priory showing the 'puddle-jumper' strip	129
Shackleton Mk 1	160
HM Submarine *Andrew*	160
The Shackleton Mk 11 involved in the Autolycus exercise	160
Meteor Night Fighters Mk 11	161
After the jet flight to Malta	161

Foreword

I had just walked into the crew room after completing my fifth solo flight, when the landing had been the best so far, and was puzzled to be told that Hodson wanted to see me in his office. Naturally I wondered what I had done wrong.

My instructor was looking at a number of reports spread in front of him when I entered.

'Come in and take a chair, Johnstone. I want a word with you.'

He continued to study the forms on the desk.

'I've just been going through my notes, Sandy, and am happy to tell you you are doing fine, so you can wipe that worried expression from your face. In fact, I see you have notched up seven hours solo on top of the eight under instruction, so how do you feel about it so far?'

I told him I was thoroughly enjoying flying and was finding it easier to cope with every time I went up.

'Yes, that's exactly what I want to speak to you about. You see, it is all too easy to become over-confident in this game and statistics show there are several clearly defined points in everyone's flying career when it most shows up. The first is around the fifteen hours' mark, which you have now reached. Therefore I must warn you about it and remind you that you will be going into battle every time you take off – a battle against the elements and the force of gravity – when every flight can be an adventure in itself. Always be prepared for the unexpected, for you will often find yourself stretched to the limit. However easy things may appear on the surface, never relax for a moment for, if you do, you won't live long to tell the tale: Even the most experienced pilots sometimes come to grief through neglecting this fundamental principle. However, as long as you remember to treat every flight with respect, you can look forward to a long and enjoyable flying career.'

Hoddy was calling on his vast store of knowledge and experience gained first as a fighter pilot with the Royal Flying Corps in World War One and later as a flying instructor to the Royal Air Force and, being a man greatly admired and respected by all with whom he came in contact, his advice was worth remembering. Indeed, during the following thirty-four years of flying in peace and war, I often had cause to be grateful for those early pearls of wisdom from, to me, the best instructor of all.

I had chosen to make a career in the Royal Air Force and, no matter whether my appointments were at a flying station, on the Staff or in the Air Ministry ·itself, I was always able to keep my hand in at flying, when every trip continued to be a pleasure, often packed with excitement and adventure. In fact, I soon found that *every* flight was a very special one which had something about it to make it that little different from all the others. But many had their moments of danger too.

I found, too, a cameraderie amongst most pre-war aviators which transcended national boundaries, inspired no doubt by the tacit acknowledgement that each was capable of taking on the elements at their own game, and therefore must be a cut above the average. In times of war, also, one tended still to maintain a regard for one's adversaries, for airmen were spared the gruesome eye to eye encounters faced by our infantry colleagues and, whenever successful in combat, thought more about how one had out-manoeuvred and out-flown the enemy than about the fellow who had been at the controls.

Of course, enormous advances have been made in aviation since my first flight in a 1916-model Avro in the carefree days when one was master of one's aeroplane and no one was master of you. In 1934, control from the ground was unknown and the only ground to air communication was by wireless telegraphy – providing there was a set in the aircraft with someone who knew how to work it.

But the introduction of radio-telephony and radar changed all that and controls, and ever more controls, were imposed until nowadays it is almost impossible to fly anywhere without having Big Brother breathing down your neck from the moment of take-off until being electronically delivered back on to the ground. Everything now seems to be hedged about with Regulations, Instructions and What-Have-Yous and one has to possess an almost encyclopaedic knowledge of International Air Legislation before being permitted to venture into the air in charge of a flying machine. It has all become very professional and, I believe, has lost much of its fun as a result. But maybe I am growing old!

I have therefore tried to recapture in the pages of this book some of the enjoyment I got out of flying by selecting a few trips from amongst the many thousands I made, and setting them against backcloths appropriate to the times and places they occurred. The events described all happened although, in order to avoid repetition, several incidents which had taken place during different flights have, on occasions, been telescoped into the same chapter whilst, for obvious reasons, I have also had to allow myself a certain amount of journalistic licence when transferring narrative from the cockpit to characters and events elsewhere. In so doing, a few fictitious names crop up here and there, but they should be easy enough to spot.

Some of the flights were frightening and dangerous, but most had their moments of comedy too and, as they took place during the halcyon days before the robots took over, I hereby hope to share some of the enjoyment with many others who did not, like me, have the luck to be there.

London   A.V.R.J.
1978

1

THE EXPENSIVE LESSON

McColl looked up as the sound of an aircraft crackled low overhead, but could see nothing through the thin covering of mist, although he had been out of doors long enough for his eyes to have become accustomed to the darkness. He balanced his shotgun against his legs as he vigorously beat his arms across his chest to keep the circulation going, for it was bitterly cold and dark. In fact, he had just been thinking it was a particularly unpleasant night to be out on the hills and hoped the conditions were not going to be the harbinger of a severe winter. McColl held the luminous dial of his wristwatch to his face and saw it was two o'clock – two o'clock on Sunday, the first day of October 1939.

'My God, he's crashed!'

A loud thump, followed by a terrible screeching sound of metal being torn apart by rocks, directed his attention towards the summit where he fully expected to see an aircraft disintegrating in a ghastly ball of flames. Instead there was nothing. The silence of the invisible countryside was only broken by the far off sound of a motor horn.

'It must be on The Whangie,' he muttered, clambering over a stone dyke and into a neighbouring field, regretting he had forgotten to put a new battery in his torch, for he knew the field was pitted with rabbit burrows and had no wish to end up with a broken ankle. He moved cautiously uphill towards where he thought the aircraft had crashed.

John McColl was employed by the West of Scotland Water Authority as a warden to look after the numerous small reservoirs which supplied water to the nearby towns and villages. Under normal circumstances he would not have been out on a night like this, but the war was but twenty-seven days old and there had been a scare that the Germans might choose just such an area on which to drop parachutists for, after all, Glasgow lay only fifteen miles away. So John, together with one of his colleagues, had been taking it in turns to patrol the area during the hours of darkness – just in case!

McColl, carrying his shotgun in one hand and his torch in the other, picked his way carefully up the slope. He was also wondering what the bright light he had seen earlier had to do with it.

Peering ahead into the darkness – a blackness only alleviated by the faint amber glow from the cockpit lighting and the irregular streaks of flames sweeping back from the exhaust stubs of the Spitfire, I of course was unaware that anyone by the name of John· McColl even existed. Many besides myself had found the flames more than a little troublesome whilst landing Spitfires in the dark, even when the weather was clear and a full flarepath of goose-necks had been laid out across a large flat airfield. In the present circumstances, therefore, they were even more of a menace. Suddenly a solid black mass loomed up ahead, when I pulled back frantically on the stick. My number was up – I was sure of it – and in the fraction of a second before making contact with the ground, my immediate thought was how sad it was for my flying career to end up in such an ignominious way, for I had grown to love it above all else.

But the gods were with me. Only the good die young, they say. The sturdy Spitfire pancaked hard on to a large grassy patch and continued to slither uphill, bouncing over boulders and spraying earth and pebbles into the cockpit, much of which found their way into my eyes and mouth. The aircraft juddered and bucketed alarmingly, seeming as if it would tear itself apart at any moment, before finally colliding with a stone cairn erected on the summit of the hill. The impact made it swing round violently, causing me to crack my head on the side of the canopy. I was knocked out.

On coming to, my first thought was to get clear of the

wreckage as quickly as possible in case it should suddenly burst into flames so, releasing the safety harness without more ado, I threw myself over the side and stumbled off blindly into the misty night and it was not until I had put some two hundred yards between myself and the Spitfire that I sat down, exhausted, to take stock of the position. It was dark and cold – bitterly cold – for I had had time only to pull on a greatcoat over my pyjamas before taking off. Why, I was wondering, was I sitting on the side of a Scottish hillside, clad only in pyjamas and a greatcoat, chattering with cold, lost – hopelessly lost – and with a damnably sore jaw to boot?

*

The expected aerial assault had not taken place, although many had feared that Hitler would strike at British cities within minutes of war being declared. Nevertheless a great many were still twitchy about the possibility of attack and 602 Squadron, in common with other home-based units of Fighter Command, was required to maintain a state of alert round the clock, day and night.

It had been my turn to be 'first off' but, as Abbotsinch was swathed in so much mist that it had not been deemed necessary even to lay out a flarepath, George Pinkerton and I thought we might as well turn in in our tent pitched alongside the southern boundary of the airfield. B Flight occupied this area whilst A Flight camped out on the other side. Needless to say, we were completely taken aback when the operations telephone jangled us from sleep just before one o'clock, with orders for one Spitfire to take off immediately to patrol Abbotsinch at nine thousand feet. There was no argument about it; one *had* to go in those early days.

Hastily donning a greatcoat and pulling on a pair of flying boots, I staggered outside where already there were sounds of considerable activity, as George had raised the alarm and the ground crews were on the move. The first problem was in searching for the aircraft in the mist but, locating it eventually, I started up and taxied to the far side of the field, guided by an airman who ran ahead flashing his torch in the air. I only got my bearings when he shone the beam on a windsock which hung limply from its pole. In the meantime George, appreciating there was no flarepath, had driven his car to the far side, when he whipped off its headlight masks and turned in my direction thus affording me two distant pinpricks of light to aim at. Using these as the datum, therefore, I opened the throttle and took off, thanking my lucky stars I had kept myself in reasonable instrument flying practice.

Panic set in as I climbed to the ordered height and began circling the invisible airfield, very conscious of the extensive barrage of balloons flying over nearby Glasgow at a height of 12,000 feet. Furthermore, the old TR9 radio set was no good whatsoever, for all it could produce was some foreign-sounding dance music vaguely discernible amongst the static interference.

'Hello Donga Control. Hello Donga Control. This is Villa One Five. Are you receiving me?'

I might as well have been calling a brick wall for all the response I got. The set merely did its best to console me with the strains of a faraway tango.

'To pot with it!' I thought. 'This is not on!' So I continued to climb, hoping eventually to clear the overlay of mist. However there was still no horizon at twenty thousand feet, nor was there even a friendly star to guide me.

'Prestwick,' I thought – 'Yes, Prestwick! If it's clear anywhere, it will be clear down there.'

Setting a course of south-west on the compass, I trundled off in that direction, taking frequent glances over the combing for some sight of land beneath. All idea of searching for the intruder had been abandoned long ago in favour of the art of self-preservation and, after twenty fruitless minutes had passed, I made up my mind to return towards Abbotsinch where, surely, they would have got the lights on and be able to get me down. But it was a forlorn hope; everything was as unfriendly as ever.

Now, of course, I was beginning to worry about the supply of fuel and reckoned it was time to do something about getting down before it all ran out so, lowering the landing flaps and easing back the throttle, the Spitfire coasted downhill towards the West until down to three thousand feet when, on pulling off the one and only parachute flare carried in the aircraft and circling below its bright light, I was able to see we were over open countryside and not a built-up area. Suddenly I could hardly believe my luck when, lo and behold, a large field appeared below me – just the thing for a forced landing!

Wheels down. Throttle closed. The flare still burning brightly. The field looming ever closer. I was going to make it! But my eyes had deceived me, for that was no field. It was a small reservoir. Panic really set in then as I pumped frantically at the undercarriage lever and, when about to open the throttle, the flare suddenly petered out and everything was once more plunged into darkness. It was then the ground rushed up to meet me.

*

I sat, shivering, for fully five minutes before being aware of the motor horn. It was a persistent noise which penetrated the darkness with its stridency.

'Funny!' – my befuddled brain was beginning to grind into action – 'There must be a road nearby!'

So I made my way towards the din only to be led to the Spitfire which, miraculously, appeared to be more or less in one piece. Only then did it dawn on me that the undercarriage horn had only been doing its duty in warning a forgetful pilot that he had closed the throttle without first lowering the wheels for, as soon as I leant into the cockpit and pushed forward the lever, the noise stopped. Also, as it looked a more inviting place than the hillside on which to spend the night, I climbed back into the cockpit and pulled the battered canopy over my head.

It was then I suffered a frightful attack of conscience, imagining I had been guilty of two grave offences against the law, firstly for having shown a light in the blackout – and what a light – and secondly for having sounded a motor horn after eleven o'clock. However I was soon brought back to normality by the sound of someone moving about outside when, on sliding back the canopy, I found myself staring down the twin barrels of a shotgun.

'Who are you?' demanded the voice behind it. 'Stand up and put your hands above your head!'

For the life of me, I could not remember my own name. My brain had gone numb again. I could only stammer.

'It's me – it's me!'

McColl lowered the gun as he approached.

'Och man, I thought you were a Jerry!''

But what a friend he turned out to be. Having satisfied himself that I was no enemy of the realm, McColl was kindness itself as he led me to his little bothy on the hillside. It seemed a sturdy little building comprising, as far as I could make out in the darkness, a small hallway – sporting a telephone I was glad to note – which led into a large kitchen where a roaring coal fire cast a welcoming glow on to a recess-bed opposite and in which lay an elderly lady and a small boy, both wide awake. Presumably there was also a bathroom somewhere, but that appeared to be the lot and no one else was about when I went to the hall to ring up my chums at Abbotsinch. I was therefore surprised, on returning to the kitchen, to find five others of both sexes and in varying stages of undress. I had calculated there was only sufficient accommodation for three and, having seen no other buildings nearby, was curious to know whence they had come. Surely they could not *all* have been in the lavatory at the same time!

However, returning to the scene two days later I was surprised, and mortified, to find 'the little bothy' was a substantial two-storeyed building and that John McColl's married daughters and their families had been in residence at the time. The bump on the head must have been more severe than I had thought.

Naturally there was quite a shemozzle about the incident, as the 'raider' turned out to have been one of our bombers which had strayed from its path when returning from a raid on Heligoland. However, the Court of Inquiry absolved me from blame, although it was pointed out that I should have baled out instead of floundering about in the dark – something I had never thought of doing. Furthermore, the Court also made the recommendation that, in future, pilots should have the right to refuse to take off if they thought weather conditions were unsuitable providing, of course, they would be prepared to justify themselves later.

We live and learn – but just!

2

PICKING THE TEAM

'Take your ruddy great boot off my face, you ass!'

'Ouch! That's my ear you're pulling!'

'Leggo! Oh, for Pete's sake –!'

The members of the scrum disentangled themselves from the mud-splattered heap of humanity in the middle of the pitch and stood up, leaving me prostrated on the ground.

The pain was excruciating. It felt as if half a dozen demons were piercing my knee with red-hot pokers and a quick glance showed it was no ordinary injury, for the joint was sticking out at a peculiar angle. Indeed, in spite of the careful attention lavished on it by a series of doctors, manipulators, and eventually by a boxing trainer who ran a gymnasium in the south side of the city, the injury put paid to any further athletic ambitions I might have had whilst a pupil at Kelvinside Academy. My parents therefore arranged for me to enter a nursing home at the end of the school term where a surgeon set about putting it right, although I could only get along with the aid of a walking stick for several months thereafter.

'It should be as good as new in a month or so,' he prognosticated – 'as good as new. However, I'd advise you to stop playing rugger, although it should stand up to most things except being given a hard yank!'

The limb seems to have been the object of considerable leg-pulling ever since!

The accident occurred at the beginning of 1934, five and a half years before the episode on the Scottish hillside which had so nearly put paid to all my activities once and for all. I was then a schoolboy, seventeen years of age and mad keen on the game of rugby – not that I was much good at it although, in true Walter Mitty fashion, had often dreamt of trotting on to the field at Murrayfield wearing the dark blue jersey with a white thistle on the left breast! It was some time before I could accept that my playing days were over but, having done so eventually, set about seeking another activity with which to occupy myself at weekends.

'Why don't you join the TA, Son? You know plenty of people who have already gone into it.'

My father appreciated how I felt.

The Glasgow edition of the Post Office Directory published annually a list of the local Territorial Army battalions, with the current roll of commissioned officers in each, and while browsing through a copy, I came upon a page headed 'No 602 City of Glasgow (Bomber) Squadron, Auxiliary Air Force', with an address at Renfrew Aerodrome. This was something I had not heard of and it seemed worth investigating. So, nothing daunted, I wrote off and duly received a courteous reply from the Adjutant inviting me to call on him that weekend. It did not escape my notice that his letter bore the address 'Royal Air Force, Abbotsinch', the unit having moved from Renfrew the previous year! The Directory must have been out-of-date.

Notwithstanding the faux pas, Flight Lieutenant Hodson made me most welcome and, after jotting down a few particulars, escorted me to meet the Commanding Officer who had just looked in to clear up some outstanding paper work, in spite of it being a stand-down weekend.

'Come in and sit down, Johnstone.'

This was my first meeting with the Marquis of Douglas and Clydesdale, the legendary leader of the famous Houston-Everest expedition which had conquered Mount Everest by air two years previously. Although not particularly tall, one could not but be impressed by his fine physique and bearing and could readily picture him in the boxing ring where I knew he was much at home, having represented Great Britain in the sport at the Munich Olympics. His searching blue eyes were sizing me up.

'Have you ever flown, Johnstone?'

'No, Sir. I've never had the opportunity.'

My heart sank, for I feared the admission would put paid to the whole affair.

'Would you like to go up now?'

I was flabbergasted, for the possibility had never entered my head. He turned to Hodson.

'How about it, Hoddy? You were going to air-test the 504 anyway, weren't you?'

I suddenly became all thumbs while being kitted out in a voluminous Sidcot flying suit, cumbersome sheepskin boots, a leather helmet, fur trimmed goggles and a parachute before being strapped into the rear cockpit of the trusty old 1916 model biplane. Hodson climbed into the front seat.

'Petrol on – Switches off – Suck in!'

An airman heaved the heavy wooden propeller twice round in an anti-clockwise direction.

'Stand by – Switches on – *Contact!*'

The engine started at the first swing and I sat tensely in the back whilst Hodson allowed it to warm up gently before opening the throttle to test the switches. The airman had moved round and was now leaning his weight on the tail to prevent the aeroplane from tipping onto its nose. Hoddy must have been satisfied with the test, for he waved away the chocks and we began to trundle slowly forward with an airman walking at each wing tip in case the machine should be caught by a crosswind and tip over. Besides it made steering less difficult on the ground, for the Avro had no wheel brakes and relied for manoeuvrability on a combined use of stick, throttle and rudder.

The take-off was unforgettable – the aircraft slowly gathering speed – bouncing – bouncing – until the sensation of motion seemed to disappear altogether as the ground fell away. I was actually airborne.

We had been flying for some time before I became aware that something was being shouted in my ear and remembered that Hodson had plugged in a speaking tube when he was strapping me in. What was that he was saying? It sounded like – 'When you push the stick forward the nose will go down –

like this ...' at which the Avro suddenly lurched towards the ground. Then up. Then banked to one side, immediately followed by a similar slant to the other side. Then straight and level again whilst the disembodied voice continued to assail my ears through the Gosport tube. This time I heard it say – It's all yours!' Near panic set in.

I clasped the stick tightly as if frightened that someone was going to snatch it from my grasp, but my first efforts at the controls cannot have been very convincing, for Hodson's corrections became ever more frequent as the old aeroplane lurched this way and that all over the sky, and it was no surprise – in fact it was a distinct relief – when he called 'I've got her' and we started to climb.

At 5,000 feet he suddenly pulled the aircraft over in a loop, followed by a slow roll to the left and then by one to the right. From then on I had little idea which way up I was, or in what attitude the aircraft was flying; sufficient to say I seemed to experience all the sensations at once, with my feet dangling in the air one moment and my head being forced through my shoulders the next. In fact, we seemed to spend most of the time upside down, when my main worry was for my wallet in case it should fall out of my pocket.

It was fascinating to follow the landing approach when it was time to come down. A side-slip to the left followed by one to the right as the ground rushed up to meet us, but somehow Hodson succeeded in levelling off at the last possible moment to make a perfect three-point landing. We rumbled across the field towards the large hangar and switched off.

'Well, how did you enjoy it?'

There was more than a casual platitude in the way he put the question.

'Fine then! Will you join us for tea in the Mess? The CO will be over presently.'

After a sumptuous afternoon tea, to which I did full justice, I took my leave with a promise from Hodson that there would be a letter in the post within the next few days. Needless to say, I wondered whether I had a cat's chance in hell of being invited to join this exciting outfit after my pathetic performance at the controls. My first attempts to be an aviator could hardly be described as distinguished. I felt flattered therefore when I was bidden to appear the following weekend 'To meet some of the officers and to attend their monthly "Dining In".'

That was another memorable visit, for the squadron was flying that weekend and many aircraft were in the circuit. Apart from two Avro 504's, a number of Hawker Harts were airborne together with the last of the Wapitis to fly with the squadron before it re-equipped entirely with the more modern Hart variant. I remember also how impressed I was when Marcus Robinson stepped out of a Hart after completing his first solo on that type of aircraft. He thenceforth assumed the mantle of a superman in my mind and I could have never imagined myself capable of such a feat. Nevertheless, I was hoping more than ever they would have me!

The evening too was memorable for other reasons, although my recollection of them grew less distinct as time wore on. Marcus's first solo provided the catalyst when, according to custom, he was required to stand a round of drinks, after which my hosts were ever at my elbow with a fresh supply whenever my glass looked remotely empty. Wine flowed freely throughout the excellent dinner. I was plied with still more refreshment during the boisterous shenanigans involving games of high-cockalorum and 'blind man's biff' which apparently formed a built-in part of all Dinner evenings. Someone let off fireworks in the middle of it all, when the room was soon filled with acrid smoke as squibs, firecrackers, catherine wheels, and even a rocket, ricocheted round the walls. Then the large mess sofa was up-ended, with half a dozen chaps staggering beneath its considerable weight while they waved it in the air in a vain attempt to dislodge a hideous lampshade suspended from the ceiling.

Not surprisingly my head felt fit to burst by the time I reached home, where I discovered that my dinner jacket would require considerable attention from the cleaners and invisible menders before it would be fit to wear again. It was certainly a night to remember – if at all!

And so it went on. Another invitation 'To Meet the Officers' at Abbotsinch: attendance at a mid-week parade in the Town

Headquarters in Copelaw Road: an invitation to a 'Ladies' Night', when the presence of their fair sex demanded a less athletic evening than on the previous occasion – at least insofar as activities in the mess itself were concerned. Finally came The Letter.

'Dear Sir,' it read – 'I have the honour to inform you ...' the gist of which told me I had been accepted, on probation, as a member of 602 Squadron and that I was to report at Abbotsinch to commence flying training. It appeared that Dame Fortune was on my side.

However, shortly after the schedule began – training proceeded all too slowly for my liking, due to a prolonged spell of bad weather – I noticed another prospective candidate being put through the same hoops I myself had recently come through – invitations to meet the chaps, myself now included; attendances at a Dining In and at Copelaw Road; the lot. Marcus put me wise.

'Some people call it a load of autocratic bullshit, Sandy, but in a small unit like this, it's important for everyone in it to get on well together and to know how to behave in a reasonably civilised manner! Hence the initial spin round in the air to make sure you have the stomach for it, and I suppose you could say the same for the boozy parties! It gives everyone an opportunity to size you up and some, as a matter of fact, fall by the wayside. But it makes for a rattling good outfit, don't you agree?'

Be that as it may, I was thankful I had been blessed with sturdy digestive organs and a tolerably hard head. Indeed, Father always said I was solid ivory from the neck up, and it appeared, on this occasion, that Father was right!

3

ALL FARES PLEASE

'Mummy, look at those funny men with the fur collars!'

'Hush, dear. They may hear you!'

'But, Mummy, they've got on waterproof suits –!'

The two passengers thus picked out for observation wriggled uncomfortably in their seats as the tramcar lurched and clanged its way along the Joppa Road. They felt somewhat embarrassed and out of place sitting there in their flying kit, particularly as they were also a trifle dishevelled in appearance. Granted it was a bitterly cold day and the snow was lying thick and clean all around, as it had been falling steadily for the past hour or so. Nevertheless it was not so severe as to require these two Air Force officers to go to such extremes of dress when taking a tram ride in the outskirts of Edinburgh this Sunday afternoon. The little girl's curiosity was not without reason.

*

As a new member of 602 Squadron, I was flattered to be asked to play in the Scottish Auxiliary Air Force rugby team in the annual fixture against their English counterparts. In 1935 it was to be played in February at RAF Usworth, an airfield situated on the southern outskirts of Newcastle, and I decided to take a chance that my leg would hold out, although I had not forgotten the surgeon's advice. The team comprised members from our own squadron and from our sister unit in Edinburgh, 603 Squadron, and it had been arranged to fly to the venue in ten Hawker Harts – five from 602 Squadron and the same number from 603 – as we could combine the occasion with some useful cross-country formation training.

The Harts were among the latest light bombers in service at the time and many squadrons of the Auxiliary Air Force were equipped with them or their variants, as well as many of the regular RAF squadrons. They were fine aircraft; two-seaters, armed with bombs, a rearward-firing Vickers gun mounted on a scarf-ring and a further one set flush with the fuselage forward of the cockpit. This latter gun fired through the arc of the propeller using the well-known, but not always reliable, Constantinescu interruptor gear, and it was not uncommon to see aircraft returning from air firing sorties having at least one neat little self-inflicted bullet hole punched through one or other of the propeller blades.

By modern standards, of course, the Hawker Hart was a fairly crude type of flying machine. It had a fixed undercarriage, no landing flaps, no radio-telephonic equipment and no wheel brakes; it relied on a metal tail skid to arrest its progress after landing, and the only communication with the ground was provided by a high-frequency morse set. As we were not carrying any trained wireless operators on this trip we were, to all intents and purposes, incommunicado for the duration of our flight. Weather forecasting was also an inexact science in those early days of 1935.

However, the weather report which Bill Grassick, our Meteorological Officer at Abbotsinch, gave us that Sunday morning was similar to many others we had received from him in the past – 'Intermittent cloud, a bit foggy near industrial areas and the inevitable "chance of a wee shower"'. The last observation was a standard feature of all Bill's forecasts, irrespective of whether we were in the middle of a nationwide drought or at the height of the worst weather of a Scottish winter. There was always 'the chance of a wee shower'!

And so we set off shortly after eleven o'clock. Douglas Farquhar, who was then C Flight Commander, led our formation of five aircraft, the other four being flown by Jimmie Hodge, Andrew Rintoul, Marcus Robinson and John

Shewell. John Hawkes was flying as a passenger with Rintoul whilst I occupied the rear cockpit of Farquhar's aircraft. In fact, this was the first time I had been up in a Hart.

We flew towards Edinburgh and circled Turnhouse whilst the five Harts of 603 Squadron, led by Geordie Douglas-Hamilton, took off and formed up about a mile astern.

All was well as we roared our way across the Scottish Lowlands, nipping through occasional cloud formations as we cleared the higher peaks. Sitting in the rear cockpit, snugly wrapped up in a warm Sidcot suit and sheepskin flying boots, I passed the time away happily enough watching the other aircraft in the formation as they alternatively sank below and then rose above our level as we hit bumpy up-currents of air rising among the hills. I watched, too, the five Harts of 603 Squadron as they trailed behind; in fact, as the rear cockpit was only fitted with a rearward-facing seat, I was much more in the picture about what was happening astern than in what lay ahead.

We must have reached the English border before I realised the weather was closing in on us. Firstly the Edinburgh boys disappeared from view; then the ground below became difficult to see as we flew into heavy snow flurries. Finally it too disappeared from sight.

Of course, being new to the flying game, and having no way of communicating with Douglas except by means of written chits which I could pass over his shoulder, I was unaware that anything out of the ordinary was happening. To me this was just a normal flight being carried out under normal conditions.

Battling through a heavy snowstorm, and having the added responsibility for the other aircraft to worry about, it was not surprising that Douglas was in no mood to take part in a chatty correspondence with me, so I sat, happily ignorant of the stresses and strains going on around me, as the other four strove to keep formation on their leader.

Marcus and Shewell were also comparatively new members of the squadron and neither was trained to 'Wings' standard at the time, and this knowledge must have weighed heavily on Douglas's mind as he pressed on hoping for the weather to clear, and so be able to take stock of the position. Map reading was now out of the question as all sight of the ground was obliterated by the driving snow, and it was much too risky to descend below our safety height with so many high hills around.

The further we went, the heavier grew the snowstorm, until Douglas reckoned it was risking too much to force on to Usworth with two comparatively untrained pilots in the formation. So, turning due east, we flew on until crossing the coastline somewhere in the north of Northumberland. Only then did he dare.come lower.

Expecting to find better weather in the north, Douglas wheeled the formation in that direction, reducing height until we could keep the coastline in view on our port side. What we did not know, however, was that the bad weather had closed in all around us.

By now we had lost all contact with our Edinburgh colleagues who were presumably battling on towards Usworth. One of Grassick's 'wee showers' would have been a most welcome alternative at that moment, for all we could see was thick, thick snow. Still I had not appreciated the predicament we were in and sat on, the interested spectator, watching the outside men as they swooped this way and that, up and down, in their efforts to maintain some sort of formation in these appalling flying conditions and, above all, not to lose sight of their leader. Other than Douglas, I am sure none had any idea of his whereabouts, as they must have been much too preoccupied in keeping station to have had any time to look at their maps.

It must have been around one-thirty when something very large and solid-looking flashed by our wing tips. It was but a fleeting sight, but it was enough to recognise one of the spans of the Forth Bridge which, by the Grace of God, we had encountered between two of the large cantilevers, which left the formation just enough room to slip through without colliding with the bridge.

Forward visibility was now reduced to a few yards only and Douglas took the wise precaution of waving away the outside aircraft. Tricky as the situation then was, conditions now made it imperative to cut the formation into smaller units to allow more flexibility of manoeuvre, and the two pairs wheeled off into the murk to work out their own salvation. Besides, we were all running short of fuel and it had become necessary to do something about getting down while we still had sufficient left to avoid having to make a dead-stick landing in these frightful conditions.

Turning eastward again in an endeavour to re-locate the Forth Bridge to get a positional fix, we once more narrowly avoided a collision with this massive structure. By now even I was beginning to realise this was not the normal sort of flight I had thought it was as I sat, tensed up, praying hard that Douglas knew what he was doing and that he would deliver me back to terra firma without damage – and without too much delay!

Whilst thus cogitating, our engine gave one cough and petered out. The fuel had run out!

*

Willie French was a man of regular habits and was wont to take his little Cairn terrier for a walk along the promenade every Sunday afternoon, come rain or shine. But today it was snowing heavily and a glance outside showed him it was lying thick on the pavements, which convinced even him that this was no day for a stroll along the prom. However the little hairy fellow won the day with his look of abject pleading so, much against his inclination, Willie wrapped himself up in his overcoat and muffler, slipped on the dog's lead and ventured out into the swirling flakes which were falling thick and fast. No one else was about. Only him and Skippy. Even the latter was nonplussed when, on stopping at the nearest lamp-post, the usual scent of encouragement seemed to be missing under the snow which was rapidly piling up around its base.

'Come along, Skippy! There's a good fellow. I'm not staying out all day in this – Now, come along!'

Willie tugged at the lead, when the little Cairn bounded alongside, trying hard to keep up with his master. Willie had heard the sound of aeroplanes in the distance before he left the house and had remarked on it to his wife at the time, when he had felt a twinge of pity for the poor souls who happened to be flying in such weather. Now he had forgotten all about them. Suddenly his attention was drawn towards the sea when he was just in time to recognise the outline of an aeroplane through the swirling snow, very low down and making straight for the shore.

Willie watched in astonishment as the machine banked steeply and splashed down in the edge of the water before running on to the shore, when it bounded over two sewage pipes as it careered along the strand. He noticed that the propeller was not turning. He quickened his pace towards the aircraft, which had now come to rest and out of which he saw two figures emerging. Several of his neighbours had been standing at their doorways and some joined him as he hastened towards the stricken airmen. The smaller of the two turned as he approached.

'Is this Portobello? I'm afraid we've run out of petrol. Can you tell me where I can find a telephone?'

By now the arm of the law, in the shape of Constable McNee, had turned up and was surveying the scene with professional interest.

'And whaat, may I be asking, would ye be calling this contraption? Och, it's a flying machine it is, to be sure! Well, ye canna be leaving it here, ye ken, fur the tide's comin' up!'

Constable McNee's West Highland accent continued as he fumbled in his pocket for his notebook and pencil.

"And could I please haff your names and addresses, for ah'l hae tae report the occurrence tae ma superiors, ye see!'

Having satisfied the policeman's immediate curiosity, Douglas persuaded many willing hands to help us push the Hart up the beach and on to a stone ramp leading up to the promenade. Only the presence of a lamp-post and a drinking fountain prevented us from pushing it right on to the road itself. Nevertheless we got it as far up the ramp as possible and tethered it firmly to the lamp-post with a clothes line thoughtfully provided by a local householder. When Constable McNee approached again, Douglas and I thought he was about to run us in for obstructing the public highway!

However, by now he had latched on to the problem and readily agreed to mount guard over our aircraft whilst we set off to telephone Turnhouse for assistance and to find out how the rest of the chaps had fared. His instructions were welcome.

'If ye wud chust be taking a tramcar tae the police station in Joppa, ye wud find an eenstrument there!'

And so we had hopped on to the first public transport that had come along – much to the interest of at least one little girl, as we already know!

We had not covered half the distance before Douglas grabbed my arm and pointed to a field which was visible between two houses in the row and exclaimed.

'Good Heavens! Look over there!'

Sitting on its nose, its propeller buried in the ground in the middle of the snow covered field, was one of our Harts looking for all the world like some monstrous scarecrow.

Hastily jumping off the tramcar, we scampered over the ploughed field to find Jimmie Hodge standing beside his aircraft, rubbing his hindquarters and wearing a very pained expression on his face.

'Are you all right, Jimmie?' enquired Douglas.

'Am I hell!' was the reply, 'It was too high for me to jump down from the cockpit and I had to slide down the nose of this damned thing. Believe me, it was bloody hot too!'

However, apart from his hurt feelings, both mental and nether, Jimmie was unscathed. Later we heard that Andrew Rintoul and Marcus Robinson had both made good forced landings in open fields near Davidson's Mains without damaging their aircraft in any way. In fact, our only other casualty occurred when John Shewell collided with a hedge as he was coming in to land and his aircraft turned over on its back, fortunately without causing injury to himself, although the aircraft was a write-off. Of the 603 Squadron boys, none fared any better, and all made forced landings throughout the County of Northumberland with varying degrees of success. One even went so far as to attempt a landing on a straight stretch of country road, when everything went fine until he reached a corner, when the lack of brakes was felt as the inevitable ditch intervened, up-ending the aircraft as it

Some hours after crash-landing on the Scottish hillside

Abbotsinch in 1934

On the promenade at Portobello

Hawker Harts of 602 Squadron

Shewell's Hart

somersaulted over the hedge to arrive, upside down, in the middle of the field beyond.

Douglas, Jimmie and I went on to the police station and made arrangements for maintenance parties and a refueller to be sent from Turnhouse and returned to the promenade, again by tramcar, to await their arrival. By now the weather had improved and our aircraft was providing a magnetic attraction for the Sunday afternoon strollers who were milling round it in frightening numbers. Fighting our way through the throng, we eventually reached the Hart which was still being well looked after by Constable McNee and a number of his colleagues who had turned up to lend a hand.

Help soon arrived from Turnhouse and a small Trojan refueller was able to give us enough petrol to let us fly over to the airfield. And so, with many willing hands eager to assist, our aircraft, with Douglas and me on board, was once again trundled over the beach and on to the firm sand at the water's edge, whence we were able to take off to the accompanying cheers of the assembled crowd who had been given an unexpected Sunday afternoon's entertainment. We were thus able to fly the few miles to Turnhouse, now clearly visible in the evening air, whilst Jimmie cadged a ride back in the Trojan.

Discussing the episode later that evening, we realised how incredibly lucky we had been to run out of fuel at that precise spot for, apart from the stretch of beach, there was nothing but rocks or docks for miles on either side of it. But a guilty thought ran through my mind all through the discussion.

We forgot to pay our fares on the tramcar!

4

HARD LINES

Nick Tindall was worried, and not without reason, for he had watched his pupil getting airborne over two hours ago and should have heard from him by now. Besides Nick had other things he ought to have been doing, but did not want to leave his office until sure that Paul Webb had landed safely. Anyone who volunteered to be the Training Officer of an Auxiliary squadron should have his head examined, he was thinking, for there must be less nerve-racking jobs for a young Flight Lieutenant to undertake! Eventually he could contain himself no longer and reached for the telephone to call his opposite number at Dyce, where a new Auxiliary squadron had been formed recently. It was early 1937.

'No, Nick, he hasn't turned up yet. As a matter of fact, I've just been through to Montrose to find out if he had landed there, but they have no news of him either. Do you want me to start Overdue Action?'

'Yes, you had better do that. No – hang on a moment – a signal has just come in. Let me see – yes! Good Heavens, it's from Usworth. He's apparently landed there! I'd better ring off and find out what this is all about. Thanks for your help, George. I'll call back later.'

Nick re-called the exchange and put through a priority call to RAF Usworth, when he spoke to the Training Officer of 607 Squadron.

'I believe you have one of our young pilots with you. No, I'm sure you weren't expecting him! Tell him to stay where he is while I send someone to lead him back to Abbotsinch. For the

life of me I can't imagine how he got down your way – he's
supposed to have gone to Dyce!'

*

'Now Paul, let's hear your story – right from the beginning!'

Nick was facing Paul across his desk. The latter had just
returned to base and was just as puzzled as his instructor.

'Well, Sir, I set course on my compass but had to fly above
the clouds most of the way – you told me not to come below
two thousand feet, do you remember? Well, I took careful note
of the time and let down through the clouds exactly on my
ETA and saw an aerodrome straight ahead, which I naturally
took to be Dryce, although it surprised me no one seemed to
be expecting me. I also thought it strange that no one spoke
with a Scottish accent. Indeed, I had no idea I was at Usworth
until you rang up, Sir!'

'Let me take a look at your navigation brief, Paul. Come
round here and show me exactly what you did.'

Paul handed over the card and moved round the desk to
stand by Nick's shoulder.

'Well, after I got airborne, Sir, I set 145 degrees on my
compass ...'

'You set *what* on your compass?'

'145 degrees, Sir ...!'

'But, according to the card, you should have been steering
065 degrees, you idiot – where in the name of Goodness did
you find the 145 from?'

Nick looked closely at the column of figures.

'Ah, now I have it! Here, look at these columns again, you
stupid clot.'

Paul took back the navigation card and studied it intently.
Sure enough, the figure in the 'Course to Steer' column read
065, whilst that in the 'Estimated Time of Arrival' column was
1.45 hrs. Then the penny dropped. He had set the time of
arrival on his compass instead of the course and, by sheer
good fortune, had found an airfield nearby when he broke
through the clouds!

But Paul was not the only one who had trouble with aerial

navigation. Indeed, if we were honest with ourselves, I doubt whether many could put their hands on their hearts and swear that they had not cheated on occasions, nor had read the wrong end of the compass needle to go gaily off in precisely the opposite direction to that intended. I certainly had although, in fairness to our instructors, they were ever at pains to try to teach us the art. Indeed navigation played a large part in our training programme.

Inevitably it started off with simple map-reading exercises when the weather was clear and the ground in sight all the time. Then, gradually, one learned to steer by compass, until being sent off on a fairly easy cross-country flight from Abbotsinch to, say, Dyce near Aberdeen, or Usworth near Newcastle, where both airfields were close to the coastline and therefore comparatively easy to pick up. Before taking off, however, it was necessary to work out the appropriate courses and estimated time of arrival, incorporating the weather information provided by the Meteorological Office, and to have the calculations checked by the Training Officer. A minimum height level of two thousand feet had to be maintained during the flight, so it was a matter of luck whether one got sent off on a day when there was little or no cloud cover. However, as ability improved, the destinations became more remote and often included aerodromes in the Midlands, or further south, both of which had a nasty habit of being enshrouded in industrial smoke.

It was in such conditions as these, then, that I set off one weekend in November 1936 to fly to Hendon, the flying base of 601 Squadron, to pay one of the periodical liaison visits to our sister squadrons. We had been re-equipped with Hawker Hinds by then – the main difference from the Harts being that they were fitted with wheel brakes.

*

'Whoa there. Steady boy!'

The farmer pulled on the leading rein as the team reached the far end of the field and looked back to satisfy himself that the furrow was running straight and true. He was proud of his ability with a plough and had been complimented on it by his neighbours more than once, a matter of considerable satisfaction, as Nottinghamshire farmers always took pride in keeping their fields looking tidy. Although the weather was overcast, the rain had held off and he had made good progress in the upper lea. He reckoned he had earned himself a short break, so sat down on a nearby tree stump, took out his battered old corncob, packed it with 'dark curly', and lit up.

It was not long before his peace was disturbed by the noise of an aeroplane flying low some distance to the east, but he was unable to pick it out immediately in the prevailing gloom. When he did, however, it was heading straight towards him and, as it passed overhead, he could clearly make out the red, white and blue roundels painted on the under sides of the lower wings. Then the sound of the engine died away and he lost sight of the aircraft as it banked steeply before disappearing behind a copse of trees. He thought he had better go and take a look in case it had come down and needed assistance so, hitching the reins to the boundary fence, the old man set off in the direction of the lower meadow, towards which the aeroplane had appeared to be heading.

Sure enough, on breasting the rise, he saw the biplane parked at the far end of the field, its propeller still turning and the pilot standing behind one of the wings. He was too far off to see what the airman was doing but, at any rate, he appeared to be all right. Nevertheless he had better try to find out what was happening.

He had not noticed the pilot climbing back into the cockpit and was therefore taken by surprise when he heard the engine opening up and saw the aircraft hurtling towards him at a very fast rate indeed.

'What the ...! was all he had time to utter before having to throw himself on the ground as the aircraft roared close over his head and rapidly disappeared in a southerly direction.

'Well I'll be damned!'

Climbing away, I took a map from the leg pocket of my flying overalls and tried to pin-point a position on the railway line I had chosen to follow. That had been a narrow squeak!

'I don't think he could have got my number,' I was

thinking, 'He must have had his head down, for I can't have cleared him by much!'

At that moment, too, I was experiencing relief of an altogether different kind, for the unscheduled landing had been occasioned by an urgent call of nature! It was not the first time the endurance of a Hart had proved superior to my own, and on this occasion I was further regretting having drunk that second cup of tea before leaving! But it had been a pretty rotten trip even before this episode, and I was beginning to question the wisdom of having set off in the first place.

*

Grassick's forecast had been reasonably accurate except, so far, there had been no sign of any of his 'wee showers'. It had been particularly bumpy over the Lowland hills which had forced me to fly eastwards to avoid the worst of it. Consequently I had difficulty picking up my position on the track line when able to fly inland again. I was sure I had crossed the border, but that was all. Shortly after, however, an area of clear sky enabled me to fix the position midway between the rivers Tyne and Solway, but the view ahead was hardly encouraging, as a massive build-up of clouds stretched unbroken across my path and it clearly enveloped the Pennine Range. Without more ado, therefore, I decided to abandon my carefully worked out flight plan and revert to the well-tried, but officially frowned-upon, alternative of 'Flying by Bradshaw' for the rest of the journey.

All went well after picking up the railway leading to York and thence on to Doncaster, but conditions grew steadily worse further south until I was forced to fly below 2,000 feet to keep the ground in sight. Forward visibility was reduced to a mile, or a mile and a half at most, as I weaved this way and that to keep the railway in sight. There was one particularly nasty moment when the track disappeared into a tunnel and I had to make a quick about-turn and forsake the benefit of the London and North Eastern system and latch on to a stretch belonging to the LMS. By now I was not only trying to keep track of my position on the map but, with increasing urgency, endeavouring to spot a suitable field on which to put down! Hence my unorthodox landing in Nottinghamshire.

Having hopefully avoided identification by our farmer friend, I picked up another railway line a few miles to the West but, having no idea which one, resorted to flying sufficiently low to read the name off a passing station. This placed me a few miles to the north of Nottingham itself, but, as the industrial smoke continued to thicken, I was soon confounded by a complicated network of railway junctions and side lines. There were several built-up areas around but I could not recognise any of them in the poor visibility. In desperation, I swept low across the front of a double-decker omnibus making for one of the towns, to read the name on its destination board, from which it appeared that I had then found my way over a corner of Derbyshire and therefore committed to the London, Midland and Scottish system from there on. Maybe this was not such a bad thing, however, for it was this line which actually skirted the aerodrome at Hendon on its way to St Pancras Station.

I should have known it would not be all that straightforward, however, for I had no sooner settled alongside this line when it, too, disappeared into a tunnel. By now the supply of fuel was becoming a matter for concern, for I had been airborne altogether over two hours, with enough petrol in the tanks for another half hour at most. Besides, I had not been very economical with its use. So, taking the bull by the horns, I decided to forego the benefits provided by Mr Bradshaw and revert to the compass, hoping eventually to pick up a recognisable landmark.

About fifteen minutes later another railway line appeared which seemed to lead in the direction of London, and spotting a station down the track, I circled to lose height in order to read the name board. While letting down, I happened to glance directly below and nearly leapt from the cockpit on sighting three large giraffes bounding across a field. It was enough to make one swear off strong drink for the rest of one's life!

Nevertheless this fleeting glimpse of wildlife was of no

assistance for, although I knew I could not have reached as far
as the continent of Africa, I was quite unaware that a new type
of zoological garden had been opened at Whipsnade. In any
case, a subsequent investigation revealed that the place did
not even rate a mention on the map I was using! However,
having got myself sorted out for the umpteenth time, Hendon
finally hove in sight and I got down, after a thoroughly
chastening flight.

When one realises the high degree of professionalism
required by present day aviators to fit safely into the complex
navigation control system now covering the entire country, it
seems incredible that airmen of those earlier days were let
loose in all sorts of weather with nothing more than a
magnetic compass and a map to guide them. Then there was
no such thing as radio telephony; nor was any control
provided from the ground. Regretfully, we 'weekend flyers'
were prone to neglect our instrument flying training in favour
of more exciting aerial pursuits, and it was therefore no
surprise that many tended to lose ourselves when caught out
in worsening conditions. However, it is also fair to say that,
because of it, we became adepts at improvising ways of getting
to our destinations eventually. Nevertheless I learned a lesson
on that trip and resolved thenceforth to become more
proficient in the art of flying by instruments and to pay more
heed to what my instructors had to say. Besides, I felt so
absolutely whacked after that flight that I took to my bed early
instead of joining the boys for a rattling good night out in The
Big City!

In the meantime I crept up the east coast on my way
home.

5

FOR HIRE AND REWARD

This time the passengers were ready for it. As the old coach approached the turn off to Mauchline, the tortured scrunching of gears reminded them forcibly that their driver had not yet mastered the art of double-declutching, and they tensed again for the inevitable repeat performance as he changed up after safely negotiating the corner. Like its driver, the charabanc had seen better days, but nevertheless its complement of trippers was in a cheerful mood as they sat back to enjoy their outing – A Mystery Tour around the Ayrshire countryside which had set out half an hour previously from the Station Hotel in Ayr. All except one. Young Willie Macdougal had not wanted to come – he would much rather have been playing on the sands with his pals – but his mother would have none of it, and under threats of 'ah'l tell yer paw on ye' Willie reluctantly gave in and now sat, tightly wedged between the ampleness of his maternal parent and her sister, his aunt, paying little attention to what was going on around him. But he suddenly sat bolt upright and pointed excitedly ahead as they rounded a corner and came upon a bright yellow biplane parked in a field straight in front of them.

'Jings Maw – look at yon yelleryin!'

'Yon yelleryin' was one of the new Avro Tutor trainers recently allocated to 602 Squadron to replace the ageing 504's. Two figures dressed in flying gear stood beside it and the elder was obviously explaining something to his colleague who was following intently the directions indicated by his companion.

'This is where it will be, Sandy,' he was saying. 'We are

taking in this field and the one further down the slope; then two more over there ...' he pointed towards the south and west where the sea shimmered brightly in the summer sun. The majestic height of Goat Fell stood out clearly further to the west whilst the square tower of St Quivox church added its elegance to the rural scene. The airmen turned round when the charabanc pulled up on the other side of the hedge and its load got down to take a closer look at the aircraft.

David MacIntyre took my arm as we moved away from the interested onlookers.

'Can't blame them really. I don't suppose they have ever seen an aeroplane at close quarters before. However, as I was saying, we hope to start up in ten months time and I will need plenty of instructors to get the show on the road. So how about joining us? We would like to have you.'

MacIntyre and our Commanding Officer, the Marquis of Clydesdale, had been instrumental in setting up a company to help train more pilots for the Royal Air Force as part of the Government's plans for rapid expansion in the face of the growing threat posed by Hitler's ever-increasing Luftwaffe. Although it was very much an eleventh hour expedient, the civilian flying training schools now being formed throughout the country were to play a vital role in the years to come, and what we were looking at now was the inception of one of the most significant – Scottish Aviation Ltd. Arising from it too was the birth of one of Britain's leading airports of the future – Prestwick International Airport.

David had invited me to fly down with him to look over the ground and had taken the opportunity to make the overture. It was summertime in 1936.

'There's nothing I would rather do, Mac, but I don't have the necessary qualifications: Furthermore I'm starting a new job next week and I would not like to let them down right at the start. But I'm most grateful for your offer – indeed I feel very flattered.'

*

It did not take long to discover that the shoe trade was not my métier as I progressed from the packing department through Ladies Footwear, Rubber Boots, the Showroom and on to the road as a travelling salesman. All the while my mind was fixed on the possibility of making a lifetime career in flying and the opportunity unexpectedly presented itself about a year and a half later when Scottish Aviation extended its activity to include a set-up for training RAF navigators in addition to the school already in full production of student pilots. The promise of a place on a forthcoming course at the RAF School of Air Navigation prompted me to remind Mac of his earlier offer, when he undertook to employ me as a navigation instructor on probation until such time as I could obtain a Civil Pilot's 'B' Licence.

My shoe employer looked immensely pleased when I handed in my notice. It was the only time I ever saw him smiling.

'Well, Sandy,' he said, 'You will always be remembered here for, apart from all else, you are by far *the* most expensive traveller we ever have had on the road! Nevertheless, good luck in your new job – and don't lose touch with us.'

As luck would have it, 602 Squadron was sent to RAF Hawkinge for its summer camp in July 1937, during which one or two officers availed themselves of temporary membership offered by the Cinque Ports Flying Club at the neighbouring airfield of Lympne. This was one of the recognised centres for receiving training as a commercial pilot and the Chief Flying Instructor, David Llewellyn, expressed himself willing to help me out with the loan of one of his aeroplanes in which to complete the night flying test required by the 'B' Licence examiners. I had previously passed an instrument flying test and, by virtue of having qualified at the School of Air Navigation, was exempted from that section of the requirements. Only the successful outcome of the night cross-country now stood between me and a coveted 'B' Licence.

*

'That silly ass Bertie has tipped the Swallow on its nose,

Sandy. It's a damn nuisance, for I intended to let you take it for your nights trip. I'm afraid there's only the Gypsy available now, so you had better come and take a look at it.'

David and I strolled to the small hangar alongside the clubhouse and inspected the little aircraft which was standing near the door. Like the charabanc, it had seen better days, but it was certainly better than nothing.

'Let's wheel it out and I'll take you round the circuit.'

We manhandled the machine into the open and climbed on board. This was the first time I had flown a civilian aircraft and was immediately struck by the casual informality of it all. There was none of the disciplined routine associated with Service flying. Indeed no, for with a cursory 'Give her a swing, Sandy', we set off, unattended by anyone, and bounced over the grass to the far side of the field. Flying clubs discouraged the use of parachutes to deter their members from abandoning their aircraft at the first sign of trouble, so one sat low down in the cockpit with one's nose at combing level. I felt more like a doomie than a pilot as we lined up for take-off, unable to see ahead owing to the inverted Cirrus engine effectively blocking the view. Nevertheless the aeroplane was docile to fly as we cruised leisurely over Folkestone. David suddenly snatched the controls from me.

'Sorry, old boy. We'll need to go down. I've just seen Charles taxying in!'

I was completely in the dark as to whom Charles might be as we dived towards Lympne and thumped on to the ground. A small two-seater cabin monoplane had pulled up in front of the clubhouse and its two occupants were on the point of climbing out. David jumped from the Moth and shouted to me to park it outside the hangar.

'I'll see you in the bar!' he called as he ran to greet the new arrivals whilst I taxied the Gypsy to the hangar door. I was curious to find out who had been the cause of all the commotion.

'Sandy, come and meet two old friends. This is Charles Lindbergh – and Mrs Lindbergh. Meet Sandy Johnstone. He's going off tomorrow to do his night cross-country from Croydon.'

'Wal, what d'ye know,' was the only comment!

It was easy to understand why the Cinque Ports Club was such a favourite with flying enthusiasts from all over the world, for not only was it conveniently situated for the short hop to the Continent, but Bill and Anne Davies, who ran the place, had the happy knack of making their guests always feel welcome and significant. A glance at the ceiling in the bar bore ample witness of the many 'greats' who had enjoyed their hospitality in the past as one by one they had been hoisted up to inscribe their names on it, presumably in the course of convivial evenings spent there. Over the years such signatures as Kingsford-Smith, Amy Johnson, Jim Mollison, Neville Stack, Alec Henshaw, Jean Batten and many others had left their mark – all remarkably legible in spite of the upside down nature of the writing surface. The clubhouse simply reeked with the atmosphere of pioneer aviators.

*

The view from the control tower was hardly encouraging. A blanket of fog obliterated all but the nearest airfield lights and the absence of wind boded little chance of an early improvement.

'I've just been on to Lympne and they say it is quite clear there. Do you want to have a crack at it?'

The controller on duty had been most helpful since I had looked in to see him earlier that evening. Llewellyn had sent me off after lunch with instructions to refuel the Gypsy at Brooklands before positioning at Croydon for the examination flight.

'It's less expensive there,' he had explained.

He had also briefed me carefully, on what was to come.

'Your trip must be done during a period when there is no moon and you must not come below two thousand feet. They will only fail you if you do!'

The long wait was beginning to play on my nerves, particularly since the fog had begun to roll in. Following David's instructions the aircraft was filled up at Brooklands before I touched down at London's major airport. At that time the weather was crystal clear and I had no qualms about setting off for a local cinema in which to while away the intervening hours until the moon went down. The fog apparently started to form while I was being adequately entertained by young Miss Garland. I turned to the controller.

'I might as well go now, I suppose. I had better not keep those scrutineer johnnies hanging around any longer or they will be failing me before I even get started!'

Two figures loomed out of the darkness, one carrying a small wooden box under his arm which he promptly locked away in the luggage compartment behind the rear cockpit. Being already strapped into the cockpit I was unable to find out what it contained as they turned back to the airport building without even so much as a word of farewell.

'It's probably something they want delivered to Lympne,' I thought. 'I'll find out about it when I get there – if I ever do!'

The fog seemed to have thickened, if anything, by the time I had taxied the aircraft to the downwind end of the flarepath, the lights of which appeared only as a dull red glow at the far end of the field. However I was now committed.

A myriad of street lights and those from the passing traffic appeared like a ghostly blur below as I climbed to the ordered height of two thousand feet. The flarepath was nowhere to be seen however, and I could only guess at the position of the airfield from which to set course for my destination. In no time at all the friendly lights disappeared and a sort of Stygian gloom took over, relieved only by the small lamp in the cockpit and the glow from the long exhaust pipe which ran alongside the combing and was now red hot. To add to my worries the 'cheese cutter' was not working properly, for every time I adjusted the tail trimmer it slipped a notch or two and sent the machine plunging towards the ground.

Although it seemed like an eternity, it was possibly only a matter of ten minutes or so before the Merle beacon came into view flashing its guiding signal about ten miles ahead. The weather was obviously clearing! Thus I lurched along, now going up and then coming down again as I struggled to keep the trimmer in place, over the Merle and on to the Bethersden, blessing those who had first installed the beacons to guide air liners in and out of Croydon. Then ahead appeared the most important beacon of all, as far as I was concerned. A continuous red de-dah de-dah – the recognition morse letter A which told me that Lympne was in sight at last. It seemed it was going to be 'a piece of cake' from then on, for all I had to do was to reach Lympne and get down safely. But, as I was for ever finding out, nothing is straightforward in the flying game for, having joined the circuit and checked that both flarepath and Chance landing light had been lit, I was confronted on the final approach by a group of people strung across the flarepath, all gesticulating wildly with what appeared to be torches in their hands. I opened up and went round again.

'What's up now?' I wondered, 'Don't tell me I've lost my undercarriage or something like that!'

Having cleared the circuit to test the aeroplane for faults, and found none, I lined up for a second approach, ready to act quickly if the flight path was still obstructed. However the way ahead was clear and I gingerly let the faithful old Gypsy sink to the ground in the brilliant light of the Chance light and taxied towards the hangar. Suddenly I was surrounded by a crowd who dragged me from the cockpit and bore me off, shoulder high, before I had even switched off the engine. A large scotch was pressed into my hand as soon as we reached the bar where I found myself engulfed in a monumental party. So that had been the cause of the disruption! The worthy members had come out to welcome me and what I had taken to be torches in their hands turned out to have been the light reflecting from their tumblers. You would have thought I had just completed a great record breaking flight instead of a fifty mile trip from London – although I could not have been more excited if I had! The scotch tasted like nectar.

'Let's go and take a look at the chart now.'

'At the what?' I asked David.

'The chart, you chump. It will tell us whether you have passed or not!'

I held the wooden box while David found a key to fit it.

'Let's see now. Oh my God –! Where the hell have you been? This looks more like a relief map of the Alps. Good Heavens!'

The aneroid barometer I had been carrying in the back of the aircraft had traced every change in altitude throughout the entire flight from Croydon to Lympne and its paper scroll was indelibly inscribed with a record of my tussle with the tail trimmer. David was scrutinising the paper by the light of a torch.

'It's OK – but just! Look at this bit here. You have made it though. Well done!'

Sure enough one of my frequent lurches downwards had taken me right on to the two thousand foot mark but thankfully I had not come below it. I had passed!

But it must have been a touch and go decision, for it was not only in the night flying phase that I nearly came unstuck. I seemed to either over-correct or under-correct every time I did a turn during the instrument flying test, whilst on the ground I hardly distinguished myself in the orals by making a mess of describing the colours of the Civil Air Ensign when there was one hanging on the wall before my very eyes, or by answering my examiner with a loud guffaw when asked what it meant to come across an airship in flight with two black balls hanging beneath it. Nor did it help when I ended up an exposition on Simpson's Theory of Thunderstorms by informing by mentor that I had heard it was nothing but a load of old codswallop, only to find that the examiner was none other than Doctor Simpson himself!

They must have been *very* short of instructors to have passed me!

6

CALL TO THE COLOURS

The freshening south-wester was beginning to fleck the sea with white horses. Sandy Mackay got up hurriedly from the wet floorboards and sat down abruptly on the stern sheets to haul in the mainsail.

'You had better start baling, old fruit. This tub takes in a hell of a lot of water when it blows like this. I'm not sure we haven't sprung a leak too!'

I pulled the metal baler from under the thwarts and began wielding it as ordered. Nevertheless more water was coming into the boat than I could cope with and the floorboards were soon awash with water slopping up and down as every fresh gust made the little lugsail heel over, letting in yet more over the side.

'Let out the main a bit,' I shouted to my companion. 'Try to put her on a reach while I tackle this ruddy flood!'

Sandy and I had gone out in his lugsail dinghy at Largs that Wednesday in August 1939 and had been spending a pleasant afternoon sailing round the Little Cumbrae whilst following the progress of John Thom's six-metre yacht *Circe* as he battled it out with his Norwegian rival for the coveted Seawanhaka Cup. It was my 'weekend off' as it were, for since joining MacIntyre at Prestwick I had become the chief instructor of the Volunteer Reserves Air Navigation Course which required working during normal weekends, when I took time off on Tuesday afternoons and Wednesdays in lieu. I had not seen Mackay for some time and we had been having a good old chinwag whilst rounding the Cumbrae and had not noticed the wind getting up until sailing out from the lee of the island. Now we were being subjected to a thorough soaking as the little boat biffed into the breaking waves on our tack towards the moorings. Nevertheless it had been a splendid day – one to remember, for I little realised then that it would be the last of its kind for many years to come.

*

By now I was living in the mess at Prestwick but, on this occasion I had arranged to spend the night with my parents in Glasgow. However it took some time to dry off and it was nearly midnight before I reached the flat where Mother greeted me in a state of some perturbation. Something was obviously amiss, for she was used to my late hours and normally never worried even if I did not turn up until the wee sma' hours.

'We've been trying to find you all evening, dear. Where have you been? This came for you about five o'clock and it looks awfully important!'

She handed me a blue envelope with the words 'ON HIS MAJESTY'S SERVICE. URGENT. EMBODIMENT' printed in heavy black capitals on the front. Inside a message headed 'NOTICE OF CALLING OUT...' went on to say that I was to report to Abbotsinch not later than midnight. The fact that the envelope bore an address I had quit two years previously, and that both my rank and name were incorrectly denoted, said much for the Post Office employees who had obviously gone to much trouble to trace me through the address of my parents!

Abbotsinch was in a state of considerable turmoil when I reported at two o'clock next morning. Lights were shining from many windows and there was a great deal of coming and going of service vehicles, which seemed to be centred round the equipment section. The Ansons of 269 Squadron had been pushed out of their hangar and some had engines running. Soon they took off for their forward base at Montrose. Officers and airmen alike seemed to have shrugged off their normal air of languour and were strutting about purposefully as if injected with a fresh supply of adrenalin. There was a fair-sized queue outside the Adjutant's office which made me realise I was not the only one who had turned up late.

Having been duly logged as reporting in at 0230 hrs on Thursday, 24th August, I was sent home with instructions to report back at nine o'clock that morning, bringing with me sufficient kit to last for a month at least. The penny had still not dropped! We all thought it was merely some kind of mobilisation plan the authorities were trying out.

We were rudely shaken out of our complacency next morning however when the Station Commander had us assemble outside the hangar to inform us that he had received a 'Top Secret' signal from the Air Ministry announcing, in diplomatic language, 'that a state of emergency existed between two great European Powers and that steps were to be taken immediately to ensure that all units were brought to a war footing with the least possible delay.' Furthermore our aircraft were to be dispersed round the perimeter forthwith and duty crews would be required to sleep in tents nearby. This was a pretty kettle of fish, for most of us had appointments arranged for days ahead – not to say wives and loved ones to think about – so it was a subdued bunch of characters who congregated in the anteroom that evening.

'Jings, I didn't join the squadron for the fighting – I only came in for the dancing!'

Archie McKellar's comment reflected what many of us were thinking at that moment.

'I wonder whether John has heard about this yet,' remarked Pinkerton. 'I hear he has gone to the South of France for a holiday.'

John Feather had been in command of B Flight for the past six years or so and it was important he should be on hand to take charge. However, if the system of addressing the Call-Out Notices had been the same for his envelope as it had been for mine, Heavens knows when he would show up! In the event he turned up the following day and thus clocked in a full twenty-four hours after me. As officers of the Auxiliary Air Force came into line with those of the regular force on mobilisation, the curious situation arose when I thenceforth found myself one day senior to my Flight Commander, although I had only attained the dizzy rank of Flight Lieutenant the previous February. John had been a Flight Lieutenant in the AAF since 1928.

Much intensive training was carried out during the next ten days, for the lads had at last realised the seriousness of the situation. A 'Readiness' state was maintained throughout, including the hours of darkness, which placed a particularly heavy burden on those who were qualified on Spitfires at night, as by virtue of their obvious additional experience, they were also the chaps required to lead the sections on daylight patrols. Time off became a rare privilege and, as it was now apparent that we were heading for a showdown with the Germans, one or two could stand the separation from their girl friends no longer and promptly arranged for their pals to stand in for a couple of days whilst they took themselves off to get married. Thus the tented accommodation was unexpectedly augmented by the addition of a cluster of caravans, after which the A Flight dispersal area became a focal point for all sorts of social goings on in the squadron.

By now we were required to wear uniform at all times and one tended to feel a bit of a Charlie walking about the streets of Paisley dressed in the unaccustomed garb. Few civilians had much idea of what RAF uniform looked like and even fewer had the remotest understanding of the ranking insignia. When emerging from a chemist's shop one afternoon, having driven in to the town to buy a tube of toothpaste, a bevy of girls from one of the local textile mills happened to be passing by. Their merry chatter ceased abruptly on sighting an RAF officer.

'Hey, Maggie, look at yon – there's wan o' they corporals!'

Doubtless any of our NCO's would have been thrilled by such an encounter and would have been quick to take full advantage of it but I, dressed up in all my glory, felt my pride had been dealt a dreadful blow and strode off to the parked car with as much dignity as my twenty odd years could muster!

The Station Commander called us together again on Saturday evening. He looked grim.

'Gentlemen, I understand the Prime Minister has instructed our Ambassador in Berlin to deliver an ultimatum to the German Government to the effect that, unless they withdraw their forces from Poland immediately, we will be forced to take up arms in support of our ally. I gather the time limit has been set for some time tomorrow morning so I need not emphasise the seriousness of the situation. I have also received instructions detailing 602 Squadron to move to its war base at Drem as soon as that station is ready to take it. At all events you are to move nearer the East Coast within the next few days and it has been suggested the squadron should operate from Grangemouth as a temporary measure until Drem is ready. Farquhar, I suggest you fly over tomorrow and find out what needs to be done to accommodate you there.'

The CO sent for me soon after the Station Commander had left. 'I want you to come to Grangemouth with me, Sandy, for you already know the place and the people who run it. We'll take the Hart over tomorrow.'

The construction of an aerodrome at Grangemouth had been another of David MacIntyre's far-sighted projects when he had persuaded the Board of Scottish Aviation that it would be an ideal site on which to build an airfield, not only to provide much needed additional space for the rapidly expanding Prestwick training programme, but also to offer an airport which could serve the needs of Glasgow and Edinburgh alike, as it is situated roughly midway between the two cities. Three months previously I had attended its inauguration when Lord Trenchard declared it open by turning the propeller of a model aeroplane in the control tower. This had been cunningly wired up to a smoke canister placed outside the main building, the ignition of which was to be the signal for a formation of Harts to take off towards the building from the far side of the aerodrome. So effective was the canister that everything was enveloped in thick smoke and no one actually saw the aircraft going over. We only heard them! Nevertheless it was a fine airfield and I knew we would find plenty of accommodation for the boys in the swell new terminal building.

*

'You fly the thing from the front seat, Sandy. I want to take a good look round the approaches, so do a couple of circuits when we get there.'

Douglas Farquhar and I were walking out to the dual-controlled Hart, the last of the type remaining with the squadron. It was almost an anchronism to have it still with us, as the unit had long ago ceased to operate the type and had been through a succession of others in the intervening period – Hinds, Hectors, Gauntlets and now Spitfires for our operational needs, and Avro Tutors, Harvards and even a Fairey Battle for training purposes. This latter aeroplane was seldom serviceable which was a nuisance, for it was in it that dual instruction for the Spitfires was supposed to be carried out.

An airman cranked the starting handle and the throaty Kestrel burst into life. A glance at my watch showed it was exactly 10.45 a.m. – a quarter to eleven on Sunday, 3rd September 1939. The weather was sultry and massive storm clouds were building up all around as we took off and headed north to avoid the extensive balloon barrage which guarded Glasgow. Indeed some of the balloons were flying from positions so close to Abbotsinch that it was generally considered that the sooner we moved elsewhere, the better.

There was no way of avoiding the cloud if we were to reach our destination, so choosing an area ahead which looked less ominous than the rest, we drove into it, but were immediately subjected to very severe turbulence. Rain beat relentlessly at the old Hart which started bobbing and weaving alarmingly as I strove to keep it heading in the right direction. Frequent flashes of lightning lit up everything around when blinding forks leaped from one cloud centre to another as if in defiance of the plight into which our country seemed to be heading. Douglas shouted something through the speaking tube but I could not make out what he was saying, although I suspected he was suggesting we turned back. However I could see a glimmer of brighter sky ahead and pressed on, to emerge from the worst of the storm just north of Alloa but, looking back, I was surprised we had got through it with so little trouble, for the view astern was completely obliterated by a solid wall of black cloud in which occasional flashes of lightning could still be seen. I called through to Douglas and pointed over the starboard combing where Grangemouth was now in sight. My CO responded by waggling the control stick in the rear cockpit.

As instructed, I flew the Hart round a wide circuit of the airfield, all the while watching for a green Aldis signal from the watch office to give us permission to land. None came, which was surprising, for the controller on duty must have spotted us by now and should either have given us the OK to land or have flashed a red to signify we should not. Having completed another circuit at low level there was still no sign of recognition from the ground and, as there appeared to be no obstructions on the field, I decided to risk a landing.

We taxied to the tarmac apron in front of the large, crescent-shaped terminal building and got out of the aeroplane. Still no one showed up.

'Where the hell is everyone?' asked Douglas. 'There must be somebody here, for you spoke to them on the telephone, didn't you Sandy?'

As he was speaking, I spotted two airmen emerging from an air-raid shelter some distance from the building. They were soon followed by half a dozen others, but they seemed singularly reluctant to approach. I suddenly recognised one of the airmen who had worked in my section at Prestwick.

'Hey, Peters, where has everyone gone? We were beginning to think you had done a bunk!'

'Och, it's you, Mr Johnstone. We were told you were Germans!'

It seemed I was predestined to be mistaken for the foe wherever I went, for I was to be subjected to the same problem of identification only a few weeks later after coming to an undignified abrupt halt on a hillside in Renfrewshire!

By now we had been joined by the other erstwhile occupants of the shelter who were looking understandably sheepish. The controller came up to apologise.

'I'm sorry about this, Sir, but did you know that war has been declared? Mr Chamberlain was on the wireless just after eleven o'clock and we had no sooner taken that in when the air raid sirens sounded. It must have been you all the time! I'm afraid we took to the shelters!'

Douglas and I must have been as popular as two pork pies in a synagogue that morning, for we subsequently learned that our flight had also triggered off an alert in Glasgow during which one of the balloons had been struck by lightning and had fallen in flames on the outskirts of the city, much to the discomfiture of those who had been watching.

What a way to start the war! Indeed it might be claimed that we had done just that in certain respects, for our ill-timed flight that Sunday morning had given John Citizen a foretaste of what was to come in the difficult years ahead, although it was to be several months before the sirens sounded for the real thing in Glasgow. Nevertheless we, too, were frequently subjected to the jitters of those early days by being scrambled at the drop of a hat every time anything out of the ordinary appeared in the sky over Scotland. The Junkers transports which British Airways had recently bought from the Germans at knock-down prices became frequent targets for investigation every time one of them flew the regular service into nearby Renfrew. Scottish Airways' Czechoslovakian-built Spartan Cruisers and Scottish Aviation's Dutch Fokkers also did little to help the equanimity of our early wartime lives. But this frustrating phase of 'The Phoney War' did not last long, for us at least, for we subsequently struck camp at Abbotsinch early in October and made for Grangemouth, whence we operated for the next ten days.

Drem was finally ready to receive us. On Friday, 13th October therefore, thirteen of us sat down to breakfast before flying the thirteen serviceable Spitfires to our new base – none other than No 13 Flying Training School. I could have willingly throttled the character who reminded us that our parent headquarters was No 13 Group in Fighter Command!

Not normally given to the claptrap associated with superstition I nevertheless viewed the forthcoming flight to Drem with some apprehension, for it was to be my first trip after recovering from a slight concussion sustained in colliding with the mountainside. Maybe that was what accounted for the extra few knots I had on when coming in to land for, after touching down, I suddenly found the Spitfire batting down the slope of the field until coming to rest on its nose in the middle of a marshy bit of ground hitherto undiscovered by anyone else who used the place.

As I jumped down from the elevated position of an up-ended Spitfire it crossed my mind that the experience was embarrassingly similar to many of my efforts to play the game of golf when again I have a propensity for finding parts of courses where none has ventured before!

7

THE TAIL-END CHARLIES

Captain Johns stood on the starboard wing of the bridge surveying the other ships in the convoy, which was now steaming slowly southwards some two miles off the Lothian coast. He disliked the monotony of these voyages up and down the east coast, carrying loads of coal from the Fife pits to ports further south, for he had spent the last ten years plying between the continent and his home port of Newcastle, and was finding the enforced restrictions of travelling in convoy irksome to say the least. Nevertheless he appreciated the need to be banded together like this, for the protection afforded by the escorting naval destroyers and ever patrolling fighter aircraft, albeit scanty at times, provided a measure of security they would not otherwise have had. He looked up as three Spitfires flew overhead in an easterly direction.

'Surely they're not changing the patrol so soon,' he remarked to his Number One who stood by his side. 'The last lot only took over ten minutes ago.'

'No, I shouldn't think so, Captain. But there seems to be more aeroplanes about than usual today. Maybe they're holding an exercise, or something.'

*

Monday morning of 16th October 1939 had started very much like any other morning as we winged our way over the North Sea, nipping in and out of scattered showers. But perhaps we were a little more alert than usual, for we had been 'scrambled' from our base at Drem some thirty minutes previously to try to intercept a 'bogey', or unidentified aircraft, which our radar stations had picked up as it was approaching the Scottish coast from an easterly direction.

The three Spitfires now wheeled northwards where we kept our eyes skinned for the 'bogey' which, the Fighter Controller assured us, was now 'six miles ahead and turning north'. Seeking and probing in and out of the many rain clouds scattered over the North Sea some twenty miles off the coast of Scotland, it was a frustrating game of cat and mouse which was being played by the three of us who were hell bent on being the first in the squadron to intercept a German aircraft in the war against Hitler's Reich, now barely through its sixth week.

'Bogey has turned due north – *"Buster", "Buster".'*

The note of urgency in the controller's voice, and the suspicious behaviour of this unidentified aircraft which had been approaching the coast of Fife, gave us fresh impetus and Douglas Farquhar, who was leading the section, responded to the urge to 'Buster' by piling on the speed until we were thrusting after the invisible target at nearly four hundred miles per hour.

But it was an abortive attempt and, after holding our course for a further ten minutes without further news or any sight of our quarry, whose plot had apparently faded from the Operations Room table, we turned southwards towards our base at Drem. This was the same old pattern we had been following for the past few days and, frankly, we were becoming suspicious that the radar stations at Drone Hill and St Abb's Head were only reporting spoof echoes all the time. Certainly none of us had seen anything more aggressive than a flock of wild geese during the several panic scrambles we had had during these early days of the Phoney War, but we accepted it in good faith on the basis that one day it *might* be the real thing! Nevertheless we were becoming a little sceptical.

Ian Ferguson who was flying No 3 in the formation was, like me, running short of fuel by the time the coastline came into view and, as we had a southerly wind to buck against, Farquhar decided to land us at Leuchars, near St Andrews, rather than risking the extra ten minutes it would have taken to cross the wide expanse of the Firth of Forth. We had already been airborne for well over an hour on this particular wild goose chase and, as much of the sortie had been carried out at full throttle at a fairly low level, our fuel consumption had been higher than normal. Furthermore it was the third similar type of sortie the squadron had been called upon to mount that morning and it was beginning to seem as if something a little out of the ordinary was brewing up. If so, it might not be a bad idea to position three of our Spitfires on the north side of the river, as there were no fighter aircraft based further north than Drem, near North Berwick, and Turnhouse just outside Edinburgh and, if someone from the Luftwaffe did decide to pay a visit, he was just as likely to approach from slightly north as he was from slightly south.

However this masterly appreciation of the situation did not cross our minds at the time: We were just being prudent and mindful of our own safety, but it sounded good in retrospect! The truth of the matter was that our aircraft were running short of fuel; also we were hungry, as it was nearly lunchtime!

In 1939, and indeed throughout the major part of the war, Leuchars was an airfield operated by Coastal Command and the ground crew personnel stationed there were trained and used to handling Lockheed Hudson and Avro Anson aircraft with which the Command was equipped in those early war years. Spitfires were a new breed to them and the refuelling procedure and need for oxygen replenishment were unfamiliar to these lads. We reckoned it would take them at least half an hour to complete our turnround, so Douglas rang the controller at Turnhouse to get permission for us to leave the aircraft and visit the officers' mess to snatch a quick lunch before reporting back to the Readiness state.

We had barely sat down at table and supped the first spoonful of soup when the station's air raid warning system screamed into action.

'Oh blast –', our table companion, a veteran of several dicey patrols over the North Sea and approaches to Heligoland, exploded, 'this is the third damned practice alert we have had today but I suppose we will have to take shelter. The "Old Man" is a real stickler for making these practices as authentic as possible. Come on – you had better follow me!'

So, cramming a bread roll into my pocket, I trooped off with Douglas and Ian in the wake of our host on the assumption that it was better to do what the Romans did when one was in Rome.

Arriving at the nearest air raid shelter, a sort of sunken concrete tube covered by a mound of earth which had a few tufts of grass beginning to grow on it, we found the 'House Full' sign was already up and that there was precious little room left in it for us late arrivals. So, to avoid completely offending the susceptibilities of the 'Old Man', we compromised by climbing on top of the mound, leaving our less fortunate, but more conscientious, Coastal Command colleagues to sweat it out in the Stygian gloom of their concrete tube.

Nothing much seemed to be happening: All was quiet as the minutes ticked by: I ate my roll. We discussed the shortcomings of the Fighter controlling system and the cocktail party we were hoping to hold in the Royal Hotel in North Berwick the following week.

Soon we could hear vaguely the sound of aircraft in the distance, but it was probably some of our own, or 603 Squadron, continuing the dreary job of mounting fighter cover for the coastal convoys which assembled regularly in Methil Bay and crept up and down the east coast to ports in southern England. Or it could be the engines of a Hudson being run up on the airfield during a maintenance check.

We could however just pick out a couple of aeroplanes flying up the estuary towards Edinburgh. They were flying at about 8,000 feet in and out of the few clouds which had penetrated this far west.

'Blenheims!' said Douglas.

'Wonder where they are making for?' added Ian.

'Must be a new mark of Blenheim,' said I. 'I've never seen any like those before. When do you think we can go back to the mess? I'm hungry!'

'I'll just nip over and find out what is going on and for how long we are going to be stuck here –'

Thus saying, Douglas strolled off towards the side entrance

of the building and disappeared inside.

Less than a minute later he shot out of the doorway as if pursued by all the demons in hell.

'For Pete's sake get a move on,' he shouted. 'These were no Blenheims – they were 88's!'

Cutting corners and bucketing across the verges, the little van which had waited to take us back to the airfield careered on to the tarmac where we found that these excellent Coastal lads had not only completed the refuelling and resupply of our aircraft, but had mastered the intricacies of starting them up and there they were, our three Spitfires, engines already running and with Group Captain Brian Baker, the 'Old Man' himself, urging us on with a few well chosen invectives about the incompetency of Fighter Command in general, and certain pilots of 602 Squadron in particular.

Of course, while we had been idling the time away on the top of the air raid shelter behind the mess, the rest of the boys of 602 and 603 Squadrons, the latter still flying their Gloster Gladiators, were piling into a dozen Junkers 88's of KG 100 which had ventured across the North Sea to attack naval targets moored off the dockyards at Rosyth. This was, in fact, the first raid carried out by any enemy aircraft over the British Isles since the war began. Subsequent records showed that this particular Luftwaffe squadron comprised a carefully selected bunch of aircrew, ex-German Airline pilots, graduates of British universities and so forth – but all having some personal recent knowledge of the target areas they were detailed to attack. They were briefed carefully to avoid dropping any bombs on land based targets to prevent casualties to civilians, and they scrupulously followed their instructions and no bombs fell on land. The only casualties were sustained by a naval cruiser anchored to the west of the Forth Bridge. However, a number of pedestrians in the outskirts of Edinburgh and Leith were no doubt surprised, and put in no small danger, when the odd Ju 88 was being hotly pursued by a Spitfire or a Gladiator at roof-top level over their heads, with a ding-dong exchange of .303 fire going on between the fighters and the rear gunners in the bombers they were pursuing. Fortunately the only casualties were four of the

Ju 88's and one Heinkel 111 reconnaissance aircraft which got accidentally caught up in the melee, all of which came to grief in the sea off the Lothian coast. Several of their crews were picked up injured and nursed back to health in local hospitals before being shipped off to Canada, where they were interned as prisoners of war for the remainder of the hostilities. Amongst them was the pilot of the Heinkel, who had been a student at Edinburgh University and a member of the Flying Club at Macmerry prior to the outbreak of the war. According to George Pinkerton, who was credited with shooting down the Heinkel and who later visited his erstwhile adversary in hospital, the main worry of this particular Hans was that his recent girl friend in Edinburgh should never find out what he had been up to!

We three tail-end-Charlies eventually got ourselves airborne from Leuchars and headed towards the scene of the fighting. Crossing the Firth I was suddenly aware of severe buffeting and, looking over the side, was alarmed to see the aircraft carrier *Furious* zig-zagging below and firing at me with everything she had. This was my first taste of the Royal Navy's well-known maxim of 'Fire first – Interrogate later', and I cannot say I appreciated it! By the time I had taken prudent, but fortunately effective, action to escape the unwelcome attention of our own naval guns and arrived in the area of the Forth Bridge, the skirmish was all but over and my own little contribution to the affair consisted of one very long range, and probably ineffectual, shot at a fast departing Ju 88 as it climbed for cloud cover out over the coast.

But it still looked like a Blenheim to me!

8

TAKE COVER

Claire poked her head through the entrance of the shelter, relieved to be breathing fresh air again after the irritating paraffin fumes given off by the hurricane lamp which obviously did not have its wick properly trimmed. The night was dark, but clear, and she could hear the sound of aircraft overhead. In the distance a number of searchlights stabbed the darkness with shafts of light.

'Let's go back to the house, Margaret. It's damnably uncomfortable in here and I'm getting cold.'

'But they said we had to stay in here if there were any more alerts. Has the all clear sounded yet? We would never hear the end of it if we don't do what we are told. Let's wait a few minutes longer.'

'Oh, all right – but never again! I would rather be blown to Kingdom-come than have to spend another night in this confounded place!'

Claire Saul and Margaret, my wife, continued to sit it out in the blackness of their little air raid shelter at the bottom of the garden, the gloom only slightly relieved by the feeble yellow light given off by the lamp hanging from a hook in the ceiling. A couple of old canvas garden chairs was their only comfort.

Claire and Margaret had been sharing a small cottage at Gullane for some months now and their respective husbands, Birdie and me, visited them whenever our duties would allow. The two girls had continued to show such disregard for their personal safety by disdaining to take shelter during an air raid, that Birdie and I had gone to work and converted the old

With Corporal Burnett and Spitfire Q

HMT *Almanzora*

La Maison sur la Dune, Beirut 1941

Cannon armed Hurricane at El Bassa with Butch Barton alongside

Reconnaissance photograph of small chemical factory at Pochino

pigstye into a form of air raid shelter for them. We shored it up with timber props inside and added a lining of well-filled sandbags to the outside walls. We even had buried some tinned food under the floor in case they should ever have to make a prolonged stop inside. We realised it was far from ideal, but at least it was something. The real problem was to get the women to use it and our patience was beginning to wear a little thin. We even threatened to cut off their supply of gin if they persisted in ignoring our injunctions!

It was mid-June 1940 and the war was really under way. Hitler's armies had already marched the length and breadth of Western Europe and now only the British Isles remained inviolate in the face of seemingly impossible odds. It was a time of great challenge and there was plenty of aerial activity to contend with.

Bit by bit we had been improving the techniques for getting the most out of our Spitfires and reckoned we could now give a fairly good account of ourselves both by day and by night as we continued to maintain Readiness states from our base at Drem. The radar cover was better, and the standard of fighter controlling had improved as the level of experience rose. Many of the difficulties of operating Spitfires at night had been overcome by making certain defined patrol points clearly identifiable by means of different coloured searchlights positioned near them. Batchy Atcherley's 'Drem Lighting' had taken most of the worries out of the airfield circuit and now the majority of pilots in 602 Squadron could justifiably claim to be fully operational – day *and* night!

*

The Operations Room had been reporting a number of suspicious plots in the area and our lads had been maintaining a series of line patrols for the past few hours. Around midnight, I found myself patrolling at 10,000 feet on a line running roughly between Dalkeith and Musselburgh. There appeared to be an undue amount of talking on the radio, which generally indicated that we were 'on to something'. The voice of another pilot came through on the air together with

the controller's urgent appeals to 'Look to port', 'Buster' –
'It's dead ahead of you now!'

'I think I see it – yes! Tally Ho!' – then a pause whilst the
radio crackled on, the excited pilot having apparently
forgotten to switch off his transmitting button. I could hear his
gentle panting and curses muttered under the breath as he
probed deeply into the darkness for his target. My heart felt
for him, for I had so often myself known that feeling of
frustration when you thought you had finally made contact
with a 'bandit' only to have lost sight of him again as the glare
from your own exhaust stubs blinded you temporarily as you
turned towards your quarry.

'Hell! I've lost him, Donga Control. Can you give me
another steer?'

The voice of my colleague sounded heavy with
disappointment. He was probably one of the Edinburgh boys
patrolling further to the west, as the enemy activity seemed to
be centred on the Lanarkshire area that night.

'Have lost your target for the moment! Keep patrolling on
Alpha.'

Inwardly cursing that my own patrol line kept me so far to
the east, I focused my attention towards the west hoping to see
something of the activity going on in that direction, but all was
darkness.

Back and forth I went, turning every five minutes or so on
reaching the extremities of the patrol line. There was a slight
haze in the air, for the coloured lights which marked the
turning points showed up like long coloured pencils pointing
vertically into the sky. The urgent chatter continued. The fun
still seemed to be confined well to the west of Edinburgh.

Suddenly a cluster of three searchlights, brilliantly white in
contrast to the coloured markers, lit up about two miles to the
north, their beams urgently probing the sky as they sought out
a target. Within seconds, all three converged to form a tripod
of light and there, glittering like a star perched on top of the
Fairy Queen's wand, sat a silvery-grey aircraft plumb on its
apex.

I could not believe my eyes, for no one had said anything
about 'bogeys' or 'bandits' being anywhere near me. Surely

the lights must have picked up another of our boys.

Opening wide the throttle, I raced towards the brilliant concentration of light, turning the firing button from 'safe' to 'fire' as I did so, just in case it turned out to be the real thing. And it was too!

Racing up to my quarry on its rearward starboard quarter, I could see clearly the black swastika painted on the large rounded fin and rudder. It was a Heinkel 111 and no mistaking it.

By now, of course, he was taking violent evasive action trying to dodge the lights, but these excellent fellows down below were not going to let him get away now that they had nabbed him in their beams. They hung on to the Heinkel like grim death as I bore down on him from behind. With heart pounding, I lined up my reflector sight and squeezed the firing button.

The Spitfire shuddered violently as the eight Brownings spurted out their lethal load, but I was overtaking the Heinkel so fast that I had to pull away violently to avoid colliding with it. Consequently I had no time to observe what damage, if any, I had been able to inflict on it. In the excitement of the moment I had completely forgotten to pull back the throttle and must have been closing up on him very fast indeed. At any rate I found myself hurtling downwards in the inky blackness without a clue about my own flying attitude. All I knew was that none of the instruments on the dashboard seemed to be behaving properly! The cross-bar of the artificial horizon was stuck tight into the top left hand corner of the instrument face; the gyro compass was spinning round so fast that I could not read it and the altimeter was unwinding like a clock gone mad! Furthermore I suddenly felt as if I was carrying an awful lot of weight on my shoulders and my feet were no longer touching the rudder pedals. This was not surprising, of course, for I soon discovered I was upside down and just starting into a screaming inverted dive!

Hastily pulling myself together, I managed to wriggle out of the dilemma and point the Spitfire upwards again towards the searchlight beams which were still holding the quarry in their dazzling light.

This time I was more circumspect in the manner of approaching the target which, I was surprised to see, was now trailing a heavy pall of smoke, whitish-looking in the blaze of light, from its starboard engine. Maybe I had hit him after all!

Closing gradually dead astern, I got all set to deliver the coup de grace. This was almost copy-book stuff!

Slowly creeping up, I waited until the Heinkel's full wing span just filled the orange graticule on my reflector sight and let him have it! He immediately disappeared from view as a mixture of engine oil and glycol flew back in a thick oily stream and completely obscured my windscreen.

Pulling out to port, I was now satisfied he was on the way down. Both engines were on fire and smoking badly. Furthermore, a glance at the altimeter showed that he was losing height rapidly.

Thus I followed my victim across the Lothian countryside as one battery of searchlights handed him over to the next. These boys had a lot to be proud of that night for, once locked on to their target, they never let it go, and it was only when he crossed the coast, low down, just south of Dunbar, that they were finally forced to relinquish their vigil.

By this time my eyes had become re-accustomed to the dark conditions and I was able to follow the progress of the Heinkel from the fires in its engines. About a mile or so out to sea he prepared to ditch and I watched the two beams from his landing lights as he switched them on to help him through the final agony. The twin specks of light stopped moving forward as the aircraft hit the sea with an almighty splash and slowly, imperceptibly at first, began to take on a greenish hue which grew darker and dimmer as the Heinkel sank into the cold waters of the North Sea. As this was my first confirmed victory I was anxious not to lose all proof of its identity: I wanted someone, or at least something, to be picked up.

Flying over the spot where the lights had disappeared, I fired off the colours of the day, a two-star red Very cartridge, to mark the spot for any rescue craft which might have been making towards the scene. The combination of colours was changed daily and a wide permutation was used. It just happened to be red-red at that particular time of that particular day. What none of us knew, however, was that the ground defence forces in the district had also arranged their own system of code signals as a warning against imminent invasion and, by an unfortunate coincidence, a two-star red signal to them meant that the balloon was about to go up! We only learned this later when two rather wearisome Army officers called on the Station Commander to complain that the land forces had turned out to a man from the coast of Fife right down to the Border itself! So much for my efforts to direct a rescue boat to the stricken raider.

Returning to Drem I was met by a delighted bunch of colleagues who had been treated to a grandstand view of the whole proceedings. Apparently the knock-out blow had been delivered directly overhead. Flight Sergeant Connors jumped on to the wing and thrust a steaming mug of cocoa into my hand before I had even switched off.

'That was great, Sir. We watched the whole thing – it was just great. Hey, Corporal Burnett, fetch a paint brush and put a flippin' swastika on the Flight Commander's aircraft.'

Batchy Atcherley was the next on the scene.

'Well done, Sandy, but thank your lucky stars I managed to stop the ack-ack boys from opening up. Ten to one they would have clobbered you if they had let anything off. You know what they're like!'

The Intelligence Officer seemed to take a long time to fill out his report although, in fairness to him, the poor fellow had been hauled from his bed at two in the morning and was taking some time to crank into action. Indeed, before he had returned from his office, whence he had forgotten to bring the right forms, the police had run up from Dunbar to say that three German crew members had been brought ashore in the local lifeboat and that the pilot had been a young whippersnapper of eighteen who had actually spat at one of the nurses when she started to dress his wounds. It seemed the time of chivalry had passed. However the incident had gone from my mind as I walked over to the Spitfire on which Corporal Burnett was busily wielding a small camel-hair paint brush. By Jingo, LO-Q had moved into the 'upper bracket' with a neat little white swastika painted on the fuselage just below the windscreen combing! Nevertheless she had been put into some most unusual positions before she had won that spur!

As soon as I could disentangle myself from the welcome-home party, I made for the nearest telephone, for I wanted to hear the reactions of my wife, who must also have witnessed my heroic deeds! She seemed to take a very long time to answer the telephone.

'What did you think of that, Marg?'

I was still excited and my voice was probably coming through at least one octave too high.

'Who's that?' was the disinterested rejoinder.

'It's me – Sandy – your husband!'

'Oh, it's you, is it. What do you mean? What did I think of *what*?'

'The raid! I got one! Slap-bang over your head! Didn't you watch it?'

And that was the only time she *ever* used that air raid shelter!

9

SOUTHWARD HO!

Webb turned over the record and wound up the portable gramophone.

'Oh for Pete's sake, Paul – not that again! Anything but that one ...'

Paul looked aggrieved as he selected the next disc from the pile.·He enjoyed his latest acquisition, 'In The Mood' – so had we when we first heard it – but little else had been played on the machine for the past week and we now knew every cadence of every beat of the wretched tune! The jaunty strains of Ella Fitzgerald belting out 'A Tisket, A Tasket' began to scratch out instead.

'Anyone for a game of Ludo?'

The boys were bored. It was frustrating just sitting around the crew room day after day with no operational flying to do, particularly when our colleagues in the south were in action several times a day tackling hordes of German bombers and fighters which were wreaking much havoc on targets along the South Coast. Our turn must surely come soon.

I appreciated their feelings for, although assuming command of the squadron six weeks previously, I had made a point of keeping myself in operational trim and insisted on taking my turn on the Readiness states. Indeed we had not been involved in a scramble for the past three days and the only productive flying I personally had carried out had been a couple of flights to test a new-fangled glycol windscreen de-icer we had recently knocked up. The Night State had just started and Paul, Donald Jack and I were faced with another uncomfortable night ahead, although the small trestle beds we had managed to scrounge from Stores provided more comfort than the broken-down chairs charitably loaned by the Mess, and the only reason we had been allocated these was because they had suffered so much damage during a succession of boisterous pre-war Dining In Nights that they were no longer considered in keeping with the dignity of the anteroom!

The bewitching hour was upon us and Donald had just relieved me of sixpence as his last man got 'home' on the Ludo board before mine, when the door burst open and Pat Lyall and Harry Moody rushed in. We assumed their excitement was due to a surfeit of ale at one of the local hostelries.

'You know that barmaid at the Royal? Well, she's telling everyone that 602 is moving south soon! Yes, honest injun!'

If the news was true, it would not be the first time this particular lady had somehow got prior wind of an impending squadron movement before the chaps themselves. The rumour was worth checking.

The Duty Officer at Group Headquarters sounded slightly incredulous.

'Yes, it's true all right. Haven't you got your signal yet? It was sent off from here at – er – let me see – at 1920. Tangmere – the day after tomorrow!'

'Take my place, Paul. And get Crackers and Mr Macintosh out of their beds and tell them to come to my office as soon as possible. I'd better get things moving.'

The Adjutant and OC Maintenance yawned widely as we pored over the lists. However, the duty clerk had done his best to bring some life back to them by brewing up mugs of tea in the orderly room, and now we three had begun the task of annotating items of equipment to be earmarked for our sojourn in the south. Manuals, log books, spares, batteries and a hundred and one other items necessary to keep us in the air.

Sure enough, Group's signal had been on my desk when I got to my office, detailing the squadron to prepare for a short stay at Tangmere, probably for a week or ten days, but nevertheless, in spite of the temporary nature of the move, much still had to be taken. We were instructed to include only our first line servicing personnel and to leave behind at Drem the Squadron Headquarters and second line crews. However I determined to take along our Intelligence Officer, for I suspected there would be plenty to keep him busy once we got stuck into the fighting. Two Harrow aircraft would be made available to transport the troops and equipment.

Having got things moving, it was time to break the news to my wife, but I was no sooner in the cottage when another signal was phoned through to the effect that the squadron was not going to Tangmere after all – we were to operate from its satellite airfield at Westhampnett instead. This was of no real consequence as Westhampnett is situated only a few miles from the parent station.

The intervening day was one of feverish activity as crate after crate was hammered together before being stacked in the hangar with others to be loaded on the aircraft as soon as the Harrows arrived. Everywhere there was an atmosphere of suppressed excitement as the air and ground crews alike bent to the task of preparing for departure. The lights were still on in the hangar when I finally left for the cottage late that evening.

*

Friday, 13th August 1940 could not have started in a less auspicious manner as far as we were concerned, for dawn saw the countryside swathed in low clouds, with rain coming down in buckets. On the airfield itself, however, all sixteen Spitfires had been wheeled out and were ready for take-off. Twelve front line aircraft and four in reserve. As always when the chips are down, the ground staff had taken off their jackets and had worked like beavers throughout the night to achieve a hundred per cent serviceability, whilst others had loaded the equipment and our personal gear into the Harrows, which had turned up late the previous evening. All that remained was to brief the lads for the flight.

'I'm afraid the weather is pretty foul along your entire route, Sir. However, it should begin to lift over the South Coast this afternoon, if you can wait that long.'

The Senior Air Staff Officer was not in the least sympathetic when I passed on our Met Officer's gloomy prognosis.

'You are wanted urgently, so get cracking as soon as possible!'

The Station Commander came to wish us bon voyage, when I told him about Group's reaction to my request to delay the flight. He saw their point but agreed with the suggestion to break our journey at Church Fenton to refuel, in case we had to make a diversion in the south. The air of excitement was now tinged with apprehension as the lads gathered their maps and flying gear before walking to the aircraft. The Harrows had taken off half an hour earlier and we had watched them disappear into low clouds within seconds of becoming airborne.

Not being restricted by defined runways, we spread ourselves across the airfield in four sections in preparation for the take-off. A quick look round and a check call on the radio, to make sure all pilots were ready, was all that remained to be done before starting our big adventure. Metaphorically speaking our loins were girt and we were ready to join battle with the enemy!

Suddenly a vehicle drew up just short of my starboard wing tip, and when I looked over the cockpit, there was the Station Commander's staff car with Wing Commander Atcherly at the wheel and Padre Sutherland occupying the passenger's position, the latter's head stuck through the open window and blowing on a set of bagpipes for all he was worth. Whatever music he was skirling was quite inaudible as the large formation began to move forward, with the staff car keeping station at my wing tip – faster, faster – ever faster, until I thought the Humber's suspension must surely split apart under the assault. The car only fell astern as we were about to become airborne, when the last I saw of it was the driver's arm waving vigorously from one window and the padre's bagpipes being flourished from the other. It had been little more than an impression, for I had to concentrate on instruments as soon as we climbed away to be quickly swallowed up by the rain-filled clouds. Nevertheless it had been a memorable, if somewhat unorthodox, farewell!

Slowly turning on to a southerly course to allow the others to keep station, we climbed steadily until breaking into the clear at 15,000 feet, when McDowall called to say he was having trouble with his engine and was returning to base. However the remaining fifteen Spitfires were soon assembled in a reasonable formation as we continued south, eagerly looking ahead for a break in the clouds which, we hoped, would turn up soon. But none came.

I had been unable to obtain a ground fix and was therefore having to rely on courses worked out from estimated wind speeds given to me by our Meteorological Officer, and these were unlikely to be accurate when translated to our operating height.

Calling the boys into close formation, I started to let down into the clouds when our estimated time for descending came up, but they must have had an uncomfortable ride through them as we encountered a considerable amount of turbulence and it became very dark for a while. However I was relieved to find they all were in position when we eventually broke cloud over a murky landscape which I was unable to recognise. Fortunately the rain had stopped.

Beginning a wide sweep to port I got out my map, hoping to recognise a feature on it to correspond with the ground below, but it was hopeless. Nothing seemed to tally! It appeared I was lost with fourteen trusting souls latched on to my machine in the mistaken belief that I, the Boss, must be in full control of the situation! The forward visibility was no more than a mile as the formation gradually tightened the circuit while farms, hamlets, rivers and railway lines flashed beneath as the minutes ticked away. An airfield suddenly loomed into view on the port side. Better still, there were Spitfires parked around the perimeter. Wherever it was, I was going to land there, well aware we were not going to be very popular for arriving unannounced at a strange airfield, with fifteen thirsty Spitfires and the same number of hungry pilots to replenish.

As nonchalantly as possible in the circumstances, I strolled into the Duty Pilot's office where a large-scale wall map had on it a compass rose radiating from whatever airfield it happened to be. Sidling as close to it as possible without arousing suspicion, I could hardly believe my eyes, or my luck for that matter, to discover we had fetched up at Church Fenton after all! Thank goodness I had restrained myself from uttering when it had been on the tip of my tongue to enquire 'Where are we?' I would have never lived it down!

We would have preferred to have waited for the weather to improve but 11 Group, who were to be our new masters in the south, were pressing us to get a move on as things there were apparently becoming decidedly fraught. So, with aircraft and crews adequately stoked up, we got airborne again, breaking into the clear at 10,000 feet this time. But again there was no break in the seemingly endless carpet of cloud as the formation flew on and on, the sky above having nothing more in it than a few streaks of high cirrus to ripple the infinite blue. Nothing seemed less like a potential battlefield than the view ahead. Eventually a large number of barrage balloons appeared through the clouds – dozens of them – and it was odds on they were flying from sites in and around London. No other target could be that well defended! Here then was a datum point from which to work and, soon after altering course towards the south-west, the cloud disappeared altogether, revealing a wide expanse of coastline ahead. It should be straightforward from now on. All that had to be done was to locate Westhampnett and get down.

To the east a number of small specks in the sky grew larger as they rapidly approached, swooping and diving from all quarters. They were soon recognisable as a Me 109, hotly pursued by four Hurricanes. Suddenly the former rolled on its back with black smoke trailing behind it and spiralled agonisingly into the ground after which its victors quickly reformed formation and began to swoop round us like voracious watchdogs sniffing at a visitor whose scent they did not recognise. Unfortunately our radios were not fitted with the appropriate crystals and we were unable to communicate with our interrogators. However they must have been satisfied with our credentials, for they quickly withdrew to the east leaving us free to seek out our destination.

Fortunately I had taken careful note of Westhampnett's

position on the map, for it turned out to be nothing more than three large fields knocked into one larger one, with the old hedgelines perpetuated by the application of camouflage paint. Indeed, from the air, it was difficult to believe the three original fields did not still exist. Nor were any hangars or other large buildings to be seen and I would have flown right past the place if it had not been for a Hurricane lying, inverted, in the middle of the area. This in turn drew attention to a grubby windsock flying from one corner of the perimeter, and further probing revealed two Harrows almost hidden from view under some trees. About a mile to the west a column of smoke rose lazily into the air from behind a rise in the ground. I was beginning to wonder what I was leading the boys into!

Any apprehension we might still have had turned to pleasure when a number of our own ground crews appeared from a hut to marshal us in, some to positions beneath the trees and others to be spread out along the northern boundary of the field. Four Hurricanes were parked close to the Harrows.

'Glad to see you, Johnstone. It's been decidedly sticky here lately and we'll be glad of a breather. This is what I'm reduced to –'

Johnny Peel pointed to the four Hurricanes with his free hand. The other arm was in a sling.

'Come and I'll show you round.'

Peel's lads had been in the thick of the fighting for some time and 145 Squadron had been taking a hammering. Indeed they had lost three aircraft that same day, one of them the Hurricane lying in the middle of the field which Johnny had managed to get down, albeit with a badly shot-up undercarriage. He suffered a broken arm when the aeroplane cartwheeled on to its back. But, he cheerfully pointed out, the smoke rising from behind the hill was from the remains of a 109 which his boys had seen off earlier that afternoon.

Three Nissen huts tucked under the trees were to serve as offices and crew rooms for A Flight, whilst B Flight were allocated two further huts sited alongside the northern boundary. An empty farmhouse would serve as a Mess for the officers, whilst another farm cottage would do similar duty for the NCO's. According to Peel, the airmen would be billeted in kennels a little distance up the road leading to Goodwood Racecourse.

While we had been talking, the Harrows took off for Drem with 145 Squadron's ground crews and gear on board. They were soon followed by the four Hurricanes. Johnny himself was determined to take his car to Scotland, but I had certain qualms about letting him go, for it was a devil of a long way to drive with only one arm functioning properly. However he seemed in good spirits when he eventually said farewell and I took it that he knew what he was doing. Apart from the crashed aircraft therefore we now had the place to ourselves and it was time to sort things out.

*

The Station Commander had come across from Tangmere and he and I were seated on a couple of canvas chairs in a small room partitioned off from the end of one of the Nissens. He had thoughtfully brought with him a bottle and two glasses.

'It is no sinecure down here, Johnstone. Your boys will probably have to do anything between four and six sorties a day, if things go on as they have been lately. I will require two of your aircraft on state every third night, but they will fly from Tangmere as there are no facilities here. However I've left you out of the reckoning until dawn tomorrow, so you had better get your boys sorted out and bedded down as soon as possible. Just ring us up if there is anything you require – we will do what we can to help. However I must warn you that we have never had a Spitfire squadron in the sector before and we don't hold any spares for them. But don't worry. We'll think of something!'

Thank goodness I had put my camp bed in one of the Harrows!

10

BAPTISM OF FIRE

Everything in the garden is rosy!

That was certainly true in regard to the grounds of Woodcote House, our quarters at Westhampnett, but it hardly could have been said of its interior. Few things therein could be described as lovely – in fact, there was nothing in the house at all!

We had now been in the south for three days and were gradually settling into the spartan accommodation allocated for our use. The airmen's billets in kennels were far from satisfactory – they smelled of dogs for one thing – and besides, there was no transport to spare and the lads had to hoof it up and down the hill every time they went on, or came off duty. The roof of the NCOs' cottage leaked and several windows were missing whilst we, in the officers' mess, had become heirs to a building, certainly not without charm, but devoid of any sticks of furniture other than an old kitchen table and an antiquated wooden Dutch dresser. So we were having to make do with items of camping equipment brought with us in the Harrows, supplemented by a few pots and pans meted out by the equipment section at nearby Tangmere. However the weather was warm and sunny and a number of off-duty pilots were taking advantage of it and sat outside.

'It's time these blighters took time off to study aircraft recognition. It was bad enough being fired at by ack-ack over Portsmouth, but when our own ruddy Hurricanes start having a go at us – well, it's getting beyond a joke!'

Findlay Boyd was not amused. He had taken B Flight on a scramble over the Isle of Wight that morning when his formation had been vectored on to a batch of Dornier and Junkers 88 bombers by the controller at Tangmere, only to have lost sight of them in the clouds after several of our lads had fired short bursts at them. On the way back to base they had been fired on by guns from Portsmouth and later set upon by Hurricanes of one of the squadrons based at Tangmere which had also been directed after the same raid. We were apparently paying the penalty of being the first Spitfire unit seen in the area since the fighting had begun. Findlay lay back and glanced at his watch.

'The others should be over soon, for David told me we were being stood down at half past twelve. We are due on state again at three o'clock. I could do with something to drink. Does anyone want a beer?'

The scene was picturesque. The farmhouse had been standing for more than two centuries, its walls now attractively covered with creeper, whilst numerous fine trees cast shadows on the well-kept lawn below. Indeed we had been told that the owner took special pride in his lawn which had been nurtured by successive generations until it now had the texture of a springy carpet of exquisite velvet on to which, the owner claimed, it was possible to drop an egg without breaking the shell. Alas, wartime rationing was to prevent us from putting it to the test, but we were prepared to take his word for it. It certainly looked, and felt, as if it would be possible.

Mickey Mount and Harry Moody came up the path, both wearing service tunics over their polar-neck sweaters. Mickey's top button remained undone, presumably in deference to the latest craze adopted by most pilots in Fighter Command. They sat down on the grass beside us.

'David w - wa - wants us at r - readiness at thr - three o'clock. He s - says he will be handing over himself at t - two.'

Mickey, whose occasional stutter was one of his many endearing qualities, was, oddly enough, always word perfect when talking on the radio. David Lloyd, himself an Auxiliary and indeed a one-time member of 602 Squadron, was one of the team of controllers who worked in the Tangmere Operations Control Room.

'Wh - what's on for lunch today?'

We sat down to the meal shortly after one o'clock. The cook had conjured up a brown sauce to go with the spam and boiled potatoes and we were looking forward to another hour or so in the garden before having to dress in flying kit and sit by the telephone in the crew room for the rest of the day, waiting for the next order to scramble. The extension bell in the mess shrilled loudly. It was David on the phone.

'For God's sake get your entire squadron airborne – *now*! We have twenty plus approaching from due south.'

The sirens at Tangmere and the nearby village were already wailing as we dashed down the path towards our dispersals. Soon the air was filled with the roar of aircraft engines as twenty Ju 87 dive bombers appeared overhead and wheeled over, one by one, before diving vertically on Tangmere. Even as we ran we could see their bombs leaving the aircraft and hurtle towards their target.

The fearful noise of screaming Stukas, intermingled with the toomph-toomph-toomph of the Bofors and the staccato rattle of machine gun fire, was almost drowned out by the hideous crumpings of bombs bursting on their targets. Pieces of shrapnel rattled on to the roof of the Nissen hut as we grabbed Mae Wests and helmets and darted towards the waiting Spitfires, most of which had been already started up by the ground crews, themselves looking strangely unfamiliar in tin hats. Zigging and zagging to avoid falling debris I jinked out to R – I had put Q into Tangmere to have a routine inspection carried out on her – and strapped myself in. Spitfires had already started to take off from all directions and how none collided during that panic scramble has remained a mystery to me ever since.

My earphones were immediately filled with the sounds of orders and exclamations being given to, and coming from, pilots already airborne.

'Two bandits – ten o'clock – Look out behind you!'

'Tallyho, Green Section. Go for the Stukas –'

'Christ, I'm hit ...' followed by a strangled 'Aaagh ...' as the pilot forgot, or was unable, to switch off his microphone.

David's laconic voice broke through the cacophony.

'Come on you chaps – do your best to clobber these blighters. We're being bombed and one of our walls is beginning to crack down the middle!'

The Hurricanes already airborne were hogging the airwaves and it was difficult to get a word in edgeways. I tried to call the boys to form up over base at Angels 2 and, although most of A Flight seemed to be nearby, none of B Flight were anywhere to be seen. However there was no time to hang about, for aircraft were wheeling and swooping all around in such numbers that it became difficult to tell friend from foe. Escorting German fighters had come down to mix it with us and the sky around became a seething cauldron of whirling dervishes intent on a mammoth gladiatorial struggle. I was utterly bemused. Never in my wildest dreams had I ever imagined a scene like it.

Out of the corner of my eye I caught sight of a Spitfire closing on a Me 110 and blowing the canopy clean off it: a Hurricane on fire swept close by my starboard side: streaks of tracer ahead made me instinctively put up my arms to shield my face: I found myself charging straight at another 110 and blindly pressed the firing button. Shouting. Noise. I ducked again when the pilot of the aircraft in front suddenly baled out over the side and immediately disappeared from view. It took me completely by surprise until realising he had come from the aircraft I was firing at! Suddenly I was alone. No one else was in sight, although the smoke of battle lingered in the air. Further palls of smoke rising from widely separated spots on the ground added to the sense of unrealism. I decided to return to Westhampnett.

Several aircraft had already landed when I taxied to park under the trees where two armourers stood by with fresh ammunition to rearm the Spitfire. Others were already on the job, feeding new links into the guns of nearby aircraft from pre-stocked drums which had been hoisted into the gun bays from underneath. A knot of pilots stood round the Intelligence Officer, who had equipped himself with a table and chair in the A Flight dispersal and who was now busily filling in combat forms. No one said much; most were still a little shocked by what had just taken place. Certainly an awful lot had happened in a remarkably short space of time.

'But did you see it actually *hit* the ground?'

'No – I had to pull away to avoid a Hurricane. But there was smoke coming from his engine!'

The story began to emerge bit by bit as the Intelligence Officer sifted through the reports from the boys. Apart from Mickey, who had not yet returned to Westhampnett as he had had to land at Odiham with a bullet through his coolant tank, all our aircraft had returned and it appeared that everyone had fired at something during the short engagement. Probably Findlay Boyd's effort had been the most outstanding as he had barely got airborne when a Stuka pulled up dead ahead of him, when Findlay reacted quickly by firing at the marauder, sending him crashing into a field on the far side of Chichester. Boyd was so taken aback by this turn of events that he merely completed a circuit and landed back on the airfield without even having had time to retract his undercarriage. Our bag of 'confirmed' victories was four, including the 110 I had downed in the heat of the moment, and none of our aircraft was damaged except Mickey's, which was patched up at Odiham and which he flew back to Westhampnett a few hours later.

Findlay was looking decidedly less gloomy.

'That was great! But I hope they will allow us to finish our lunch next time. It was a most uncivilised time to call!'

I drove to Tangmere that evening to find out how they had fared over there. Turning off the main road it was immediately apparent that the station had taken a heavy pounding. Bomb craters straddled the gates and long fingers of smoke reached into the sky from the shattered remains of numerous buildings. Groups of airmen were wandering about with dazed expressions, obviously deeply affected by the ordeal they had just come through. The crews manning the Bofors anti-aircraft guns still crouched behind their weapons, alert and ready for a follow-up raid should Jerry decide to ram home his advantage. The gunners were naturally jubilant too, for at least one of the raiders had been accounted for by these excellent fellows during those hectic few minutes.

The scene outside the officers' mess defied description. The west wing had received a direct hit and the erstwhile immaculate lawn was now littered with its debris – bricks and plaster intermingled with bits of bedroom furniture and items of personal kit belonging to its occupants. The incongruous sight of a pair of pyjamas draped over the top branches of a flowering cherry vied with the equally ridiculous carpet of shirts, underclothing and bed linen strewn outside the dining room window. Some of the residents were rummaging around in search of their belongings whilst others were grouped round the Station Commander who stood in the middle of the lawn with a glass in his hand and a parrot perched on his left shoulder.

'Order yourself a drink, Johnstone. At least the bar is still working! How did you get on over the way?'

I told Jack Boret about our efforts and how we had literally been caught at lunch with our pants down. When I related the story of Findlay's encounter with the Stuka he laughed so heartily that it triggered off the parrot into giving a screeching imitation of a diving Ju 87 – so real, in fact, that several present started for the nearest place of shelter in the mistaken belief that another Jerry bomber had crept up on them unawares.

'Oh, shut up, Percy – for Gawd's sake!'

The parrot glared stonily at Jack and immediately gave vent to an even more brilliant imitation.

'Take this ruddy bird away and put him back in his cage, Willie. He can thank his lucky stars he is not fit for the pot!'

Willie Rhodes-Moorhouse lifted the offender on his finger and made for the front door. The bird was clearly delighted with his performance and disappeared from view preening his under-feathers for all he was worth.

'I think you should take a look at the hangars, Johnstone. Your aircraft was in for servicing, was it not? I don't know how it has fared, but there has been a devil of a lot of damage done over there. Oh, by the way, a signal came in in the middle of it all to say that your move to Westhampnett has been made permanent. The rest of your outfit should be with you on Tuesday. Glad to welcome you on board!'

I accompanied Tommy Thomson, the Station Adjutant, to the airfield where the damage was indeed great. The three large hangars were in ruins and occasional wisps of smoke still rose from all three.

'I think your aeroplane was in that one. Let's take a look.'

Clambering over heaps of masonry and splintered beams I came upon LO-Q, covered in powdery dust, its back shattered by a heavy metal cross-strut which had crashed down on top of it. I must confess to a lump in the throat as I thought of all we had been through together. One builds up quite a lot of affection even for a simple mass of metal! Obviously Q was only fit for the breaker's yard.

Heaps of debris lay everywhere. As yet no attempt had been made to clear it away as most personnel were still too stunned by recent events to react rationally but, in the days which followed, a pattern of their behaviour while under fire emerged, when it appeared that, whilst some had been totally numbed by the onslaught, others had reacted differently and there were many tales of heroism, often perpetuated by those one would have least expected. Such a hero had been our own squadron medical officer who had happened to be on the station when the fun began, when his Herculean efforts in rescuing and treating the victims during the raid later earned him the award of a Military Cross.

Tommy and I continued to wander around the ruins. The remains of Billy Fiske's Hurricane still lay in the middle of the airfield while its gallant pilot was fighting a losing battle for his life in the Station Sick Quarters. We came upon a huge metal hangar door lying flat on the ground. Tommy got down on hands and knees to peer beneath it.

'Gee whiz! My new Triumph Dolomite is under there!'

There was clearly much to be said for the minor discomforts of Westhampnett!

11

THE AGE OF CHIVALRY

'*Allez vous en, mes braves!* You have had enough to drink this evening.'

'*Ja, meine liebe,* we were just about to leave. We have work to do tomorrow. *Danke, Madame, und gute nacht.*'

Madame Pluvet looked round her bar which, surprisingly, had become a regular haunt for off-duty aircrews from the bomber squadron recently arrived at the nearby airfield of Orleans/Bricy after undergoing an extensive refit somewhere deep inside Germany. She had long since learned to curb her curiosity about such matters and never enquired whence they had come. However she thought they were a much nicer bunch of lads than their predecessors, but she was still not prepared to admit she liked them. Indeed, Madame Pluvet resented the presence of all Germans ever since that time in May when they had taken her husband away in the middle of the night shortly after the conquerors strutted into her village. She had not heard from Pierre since, but the rumour had got around that he, along with several hundred other menfolk from the surrounding district, had been put into a labour camp and was suffering considerable hardship in the pretence of working for the greater glory of the Fatherland.

One by one the grey-clad airmen bade her 'Goodnight' as they rose from their tables and went out into the night. Helmut looked up at the sky.

'It will be good for tomorrow, *ja.* We go for briefing at ten, is it so?'

Wilhelm nodded assent. He got on well with his captain and a strong bond of friendship had grown up between himself and Oberst Schwenhart during their training together in KG 77. Willi reckoned his captain was by far the best pilot in the squadron and hoped his own prowess as a navigator came up to the standard required of him. At any rate they worked well together as a team and both had recently received a decoration from the hands of the Generalfeldmarschall himself. They crossed the road to join the others who were waiting for a lorry to ferry them back to their base.

Helmut and Willi parted company outside the barrack block in which the former had a room to himself. Willi had to share one with five others in another building. There was a chill in the air and Helmut closed the window before sitting down to write a letter to his mother in Hamburg. He was looking forward to seeing her soon, he wrote, for the Major had promised to let him take leave whenever he had completed three more sorties.

Helmut considered himself one of the 'young veterans' of his force for he had now completed twenty-five trips over targets in Western Europe and more recently over England and, although several of his colleagues had been shot down during this period, he had always managed to bring his Ju 88 back to base. On one occasion however he had had a narrow escape when nearly succumbing to a Spitfire which had attacked from underneath, and had only avoided serious damage when one of the escorting Messerschmitts drove off the attacker. But he was not a chap given to worrying about the past. He put down his pen and prepared for bed.

*

It was well into September 1940 and the weather was changeablè. In many ways this was a relief after the long spells of glorious sunshine of the summer months which had allowed the Luftwaffe to mount large forces against targets throughout southern England, and later concentrating on the capital itself. Nevertheless we were still being ordered off several times daily to tackle sporadic marauders, and now we were climbing at full throttle towards Horsham, where we had been instructed to patrol at 20,000 feet.

'Tally-ho, Villa Leader. Bandits at two o'clock!'

Ritchie's call directed my attention towards the east where, sure enough, an untidy gaggle of aircraft could be seen making for a distant bank of clouds. They were soon recognisable as Dornier 17's when their long pencil-shaped fuselages glinted in the sun. Detailing A Flight to attack from below, I would lead B Flight into the attack from above.

However, before we could reach the area, all hell was let loose when the formation of Dorniers was suddenly split asunder by a squadron of Hurricanes which seemed to have appeared from nowhere, after which the Jerries scattered in all directions. It had been a well-executed attack and was thrilling to watch. Of course, we got our pickings.

As usual in these circumstances, the squadron went off in pairs to chase their quarries hither and thither. I soon had a Dornier in my sights but, before getting within firing range, its crew of three baled out, leaving their aircraft to the mercy of my guns. I was feeling very pleased with myself. Too pleased, as it turned out, for I had failed to spot the escort Me 109 coming up behind, and it was only when it flashed past my starboard side with smoke streaming from it that I realised he had been chased off by the Spitfire whose pilot was covering my tail. I made a mental note to buy my saviour a large measure of scotch for his timely effort!

Calling the boys to re-form over Mayfield, we set off in pursuit of the remaining Dorniers which were now in full retreat towards the Channel, doubtless at full throttle. At any rate it turned out to be a long stern-chase and it was ages before we began to close with the stragglers. I was suddenly aware of land ahead and realised the coast of France was coming rapidly nearer. To my further dismay another batch of 109's was climbing towards us, having presumably taken off to escort their frightened colleagues home. They must have been some of the new 109F's, for they were climbing astonishingly fast and we soon found ourselves in the thick of it, with a melee of aircraft wheeling and swooping in all directions. Off to the left I saw Glyn Ritchie being set upon by a 109, in the course of which his instrument panel was shot away before Sergeant Proctor intervened and drove off his adversary.

After a few more passes at one another, the Spitfires and Messerschmitts parted company and went their separate ways, both sides believing that justice had been done! As far as we were concerned our ammunition was also exhausted and so we lost no time returning to Westhampnett, escorting Glyn in to land minus his instrument panel.

'Goodness – it's only half past ten! I feel as if I had been at it all day! Let's hope they will leave us in peace this afternoon, for I could do with a good sleep.'

Pat Lyall was not the only one who could have done with a rest. Indeed, most of us had been living on our nerves over these past few weeks after 'Invasion Alert One' had been declared, as we were not allowed to leave the dispersal area. We were actually missing the comparative discomforts of the mess! Now it was not uncommon to see the fellows drop off to sleep in chairs as soon as they landed and had taken off their flying clobber. Some even curled up on the floor and dozed straight off.

'All we can do, I fear, is to keep our fingers crossed and hope for the best!'

*

Meanwhile in Orleans, Helmut and his crews were walking out to their aircraft, having attended the pre-flight briefing which the CO had given himself that morning. Major Debratz had stressed the importance of their target – the Supermarine Works sited not far from Southampton – for, he had told them, the Commander-in-Chief, Luftflotte 3, was most concerned to find that the British fighter strength seemed to be on the increase, in spite of what he had been told by his intelligence officers. Supermarine was still turning out large numbers of Spitfires and it was essential to cut off this source of supply if the Fuehrer's plans for the invasion of England were to have any chance of success. Schwenhart checked his watch with that of his navigator. It was twelve fifteen precisely.

'The weather is good for the flight today, Willi. Plenty of cloud. I hope our escort will keep up with us. We will make for The Needles first. There will be less flak that way.'

They climbed aboard the Ju 88 and strapped themselves in. Helmut was inwardly cursing the bulky holster strapped round his middle as it created an uncomfortable bulge under the safety straps. However his Commanding Officer insisted on his crews always carrying their personal weapons on flights over England in case they should be forced to come down and have to defend themselves from the wrath of the locals. He had heard stories of crews being set upon by angry farmhands armed with pitchforks after they had come down on British soil. He had also heard that captured airmen always hoped they would be taken into custody by the military or by the police as quickly as possible. So Helmut eased the bulk of the Luger beneath the constriction of the harness and adjusted the knot of his orange scarf. His mother had given him the neckwear when he first joined up and he always wore it when flying. He was sure it brought him luck.

The field at Orleans/Bricy reverberated under the throaty roar of fifteen Ju 88's as they taxied to the take-off point. Helmut looked to his left and saw that his friend Richter would be flying next to him. He was pleased about this, for he knew Richter would keep close station and thus they could offer more concentrated fire power in the event of attack by British fighters. The formation gathered speed rapidly and soon all fifteen aircraft were airborne and turning on to their first course for The Needles.

*

Paddy Barthropp seized the telephone and listened intently to the instructions coming through from the Ops Room.

'Villa Squadron – *scramble* – The Needles – Angels one-five.'

Paddy repeated the message in a loud voice as it was coming through, pressing the alarm bell at the same time. Newspapers and magazines were tossed aside as the lads grabbed their helmets and ran outside where the ground crews were waiting, standing on the wings to help them secure the safety straps. In no time at all, twelve Spitfires taxied out, to turn quickly for take-off. A glance at my watch showed we were all airborne exactly one minute and thirty seconds after receiving the order. The boys had not been slow to shake off the effects of their catnaps!

'Ten plus bandits approaching the Isle of Wight from the south-east – steer one-niner-zero.'

The Controller, like our pilots, was well versed in the procedures. No sound of stress in his voice. Unruffled. Matter-of-fact. We wheeled towards the south.

'Tally-ho. Bandits at eleven o'clock!'

Fifteen Ju 88's were sweeping towards us, scudding in and out of the scattered clouds. From our point of view it had been a fine piece of controlling by the Tangmere chap, for we were ideally positioned two thousand feet above the raiders and with the sun at our backs. We dived to attack.

'*Achtung – Achtung. Schpitfeuren – Achtung, Schpitfeuren!*'

Helmut recognised the voice of Richter.

'Close up immediately – where are our escorts?'

The only part of the message intelligible to us had been the initial agonised warning of 'Look out – Spitfires'. By some strange quirk both sides were using the same radio frequency and we were about to join battle in the verbal, as well as in the purely physical sense. The Ju 88's scattered for cover as soon as our presence was noticed, for the escorts had failed to show up.

Selecting the leader of a pair which had remained together when the formation broke up, I withheld fire until he was well within range and then pressed the firing button. Immediately the port engine exploded and the wing parted company with the fuselage. I only saw one fellow get out as the Junkers disappeared below me in a series of flick rolls.

When the canopy shattered into a thousand fragments, the violent inrush of air tore the mask from his face when Helmut turned to shout to his companion. He had barely time to notice that Willi was slouched over his map with blood pouring from a wounded shoulder before the aircraft lurched violently to port and went into an uncontrollable spin. Another quick glance made him realise the port wing had broken off at the root. It was time to get out.

Helmut became completely disoriented as he somersaulted through the air, tumbling wildly as he struggled to find the rip-cord. A sudden jerk on his shoulders assured him the canopy had opened. He was surprised how peaceful it had become as he floated gently down. He looked around him, expecting to see aircraft overhead, but the sky was empty. Turning to look over his shoulder he was relieved to see that he was being blown towards the coastline of Selsey Bill, for he was not a good swimmer and did not like the sea. Helmut bent his knees as the ground rushed up to meet him.

*

I was dressing to go out for dinner when the call came through. It was the Station Commander on the telephone.

'We have one of the Jerry pilots in the Guard Room, Sandy, and he seems very anxious to meet whoever shot him down. I don't know whether he is from your 88 or not but, if you can spare the time, would you care to drop in some time this evening?'

Naturally I was curious to see what one of the enemy looked like, for I had not met any of the Luftwaffe fellows – I had only heard about them – and here was my chance.

I was therefore surprised to be confronted by a fresh-faced youngster of nineteen or thereabouts, still looking remarkably tidy in a leather jacket and flying boots. He stood up as I entered the cell. With a click of his heels he announced

'Helmut Schwenhart!'

He inclined his head in my direction.

The interpreter told me that this was Hauptman Helmut Schwenhart of KG 77 and went on to explain that the prisoner had expressed a wish to meet his adversary. Furthermore he seemed most anxious that I should accept some items of his flying kit as a memento of the occasion! Thus I found myself the unexpected recipient of a brown leather holster containing a fine Luger automatic, a Luftwaffe pilot's flying helmet bearing a name tag inscribed 'H. Schwenhart', a German Mae-West and an ersatz velvet scarf which, of course, was coloured bright orange.

Maybe the age of chivalry is not entirely a thing of the past after all.

12

THE DEFENDERS

The Scottish climate was living up to its reputation.

It was cold – bitterly cold – with temperatures well below freezing and a strong northerly wind was penetrating even the mats, blankets and rolled-up newspapers the lads had stuffed round the cracks of the doors and windows in the Old Mill.

'Jeezus! Is it always as cold as this up here?'

Jake Edy was a Canadian and accustomed to living in sub-zero conditions.

'My mother would have a fit if she could see me now! Say, how about pouring more paraffin into that ruddy stove. I don't know what you call that stuff you try to burn in it – it sure doesn't behave like coal!'

The fellows in the 'readiness' flight sat disconsolately round the old iron stove, wrapped up in every piece of flying kit they could lay their hands on in an attempt to combat the Arctic conditions. In spite of constant prodding, the offending piece of ironmongery could produce no more than a lot of dark grey smoke, much of which was finding its way into the crew room.

No 602 Squadron had returned to Scotland just before Christmas – a thoughtful gesture on the part of the Powers That Be who considered we had done well enough during our hectic stay at Westhampnett to justify a return to our native land in time for the festive season. Although there had been a considerable turnround of aircrews during our sojourn in the south, and few of the original Scots remained, the majority of the ground staff, who came from Glasgow and round about, were still with us and, generally speaking, the new location had been much appreciated.

After the hurly-burly of the Battle of Britain, our role at Prestwick seemed comparatively tame. Nevertheless we were doing a lot of flying, mostly on training fresh pilots who had been posted in to replace some of the stalwarts who had gone elsewhere. Findlay Boyd and Mickey Mount were now commanding their own fighter squadrons, whilst Donald Jack was incarcerated in Group Headquarters near Newcastle. Only Paul Webb and Glyn Ritchie remained of the pre-war 'Old Brigade'. But the weather had turned very cold and the boys' main preoccupation these days had been in trying to keep themselves warm.

Conditions in my own office were no better, for the stove there obviously had been stoked with the same non-combustible material as that in the crew room and I had not even suggested that my visitor should remove his overcoat.

General Walker's appointment to command the South-West District, Scottish Home Guard, had been announced recently and I was interested to meet this veteran of World War One. I was immediately struck by his purposeful manner and he was clearly delighted to be back in harness, albeit only as master of a large number of irregulars – successors to the worthy members of the Local Defence Volunteers.

'For some time I've been anxious to organise a training exercise for my fellows, Johnstone; something really worth while. Well, when I called to meet Lister the other day, he offered to take part in one with his chaps and this was the very opportunity I had been waiting for. What I have in mind is to set up a target, say in Troon or Ardrossan, and to organise the Home Guard to defend it against an attack laid on by the Commandos. Now this is where I hope you will come in, for I will need air reconnaissance. I realise, of course, that your Spitfires may not be ideal for the task, but we want the exercise to be as realistic as possible and these Commando fellows will be up to all manner of tricks, y'know. They're a tough bunch. Have you met any of them?'

I told General Walker that I had. In fact Colonel Lister and I had dined together two nights previously when I had been much impressed by him and his officers. They had recently returned from a highly successful, and much publicised, raid on the Norwegian island of Lofoten when they had put the Germans' noses much out of joint.

'Of course, General, we would be delighted. I will arrange for at least one aircraft to patrol the area throughout and I suggest we lend you one of our ground sets so that we will be able to speak directly to your Headquarters from the air. My aircrews will be glad of a respite from their never-ending training programme in any case. Would you care to come across to the mess? This place is like an ice-box!'

The Old Mill at Prestwick airfield had been allocated as a dispersal for the squadron. No one could say for how many centuries it had been standing, but it was certainly very old. Nor could anyone remember when it had last functioned as a mill, although a small stream still flowed past its walls. Since the turn of the century at least, it had been used by a local farmer as a storehouse for crops and farm machinery and, for good measure, a large chicken run had been constructed alongside.

Shortly before we had arrived, apparently, one of the Scottish Aviation twin-engined Fokkers, with forty navigation students on board, had failed to get airborne and had ploughed into the hen run when, it is said, the only thing which took off were the chickens! A large jagged hole in the wire-mesh fence bore evidence of the incident although all other signs of it had been cleared away.

Ten days after the General's visit, the weather, as if to atone for the misery it had caused in the past, suddenly turned quite warm and we were beginning to look forward to our participation in Exercise Ardrossan. I had attended the main briefing at the General's Headquarters when he had explained to those present that the dock area in Ardrossan was to be the target to be defended against the forces led by Colonel Lister. The Commando troops would mount their assault from a base in Glasgow and all Home Guard districts in Renfrewshire and North Ayrshire would be alerted. The wireless set had been installed and a quick test flight confirmed it was working satisfactorily.

*

Willie Burns was careful to shut the gate when they went into the top pasture, for although Mr McCrae's cattle were still confined to their winter quarters down in the farm, several sheep were grazing in the field. He and Maggie continued to stroll up the slope, holding hands as they made their way towards the old shed.

They were happy that the weather was being kind to them, for at least they had been able to get out together instead of having to share the parlour with her folks, as they had been forced to do on the past two Sundays when icy conditions had kept them indoors. Willie was on two weeks' leave from the Army and was due to rejoin his unit at Maryhill Barracks the next day. There was not much for young people to do in Uplawmoor on Sundays.

'We'll get married as soon as the war's over, Maggie. I promise you. I'll get a job with Coates' and we'll save up to buy a wee flat in Paisley. You'd like that, wouldn't you?'

The girl sighed and snuggled close to her fiancé. It had been good to have him home for these two weeks and for once they had managed to elude the eagle eye of her mother and were looking forward to spending an hour alone in the little hut they had come upon while out walking during Willie's previous furlough. The ramshackle building appeared to have been deserted for many years and it had provided them with a haven of privacy unobtainable in Maggie's overcrowded home. Suddenly a figure in khaki approached them with arm upraised.

'Ye canna come by here. D'ye no ken there's a war on? We're in the middle of big manoeuvres and ah've orders nae tae let onyone come past!'

As Maggie and Willie turned to retrace their steps, they caught sight of a number of other soldiers spread out along a ridge whence they could look down on the valley below. The soldier was joined by a corporal who shouted after the retreating couple.

'Hey youse two, come back here a meenut. Whit are ye daein' up here?'

Willie stammered out that they meant no harm. He and his fiancée were merely out walking and were intending to rest awhile in the shed before going on. The corporal's eyes were twinkling.

'Och aye then. Well, go ahead, but dinna let on that ye were here. By the way, have ye seen ony ither sodgers aboot?'

Having replied in the negative, Willie thanked the corporal and turned towards the hut. The last thing he and Maggie had any intention of doing was to let *anyone* know where they had been!

Meanwhile near Kilbarchan, Peter McQueen and his son were peering into a hedge where the former had just spotted a hedge-sparrow's nest set amongst the leafless branches. As he pulled aside the briar to take a closer look he was surprised to find the field beyond full of troops making towards a copse of trees on the far side. A Spitfire flew low over their heads, making the boy look up. To his surprise he also saw two large barrage balloons drifting high up in the sky.

'Jings, Dad, look at the balloons. Where have they come from?'

'I guess they must have broken loose, son. They're probably from Glasgow. I wonder what's going on!'

*

Glyn Ritchie was first to patrol the general area of the exercise. I had briefed him to fly high enough to avoid disturbing churchgoers, and indeed to avoid going near churches altogether if he saw them in time. But it had been a fruitless search and he had returned without sighting any of the attacking force. It was the same with Edy – they were nowhere to be seen, although he reported that he had come across a couple of balloons drifting in a south-westerly direction. A call to the controller at Turnhouse confirmed that they had broken loose from a site near Glasgow, their crews having apparently forgotten to secure them properly before letting out the cable. Would we please have them destroyed before they came down and dragged their cables over the electrical grid system?

This was a nuisance, for we had tackled these things before and had found them difficult to dispose of. To begin with it was necessary to remove all incendiary bullets from the ammunition tanks to avoid setting the hydrogen-filled envelopes on fire. Secondly it was essential to approach them from underneath before firing to prevent shooting into the ground, but insufficient gas came out if they were only punctured in the tummy. Glynn said he would come with me. He would tackle one of the monstrosities whilst I tried to deal with the other. We would resume the reconnaissance patrols when the task was completed.

The balloons were clearly visible soon after take-off, glinting brightly in the afternoon sun. They had reached a height of 13,000 feet by the time Glyn and I caught up with them and were rapidly approaching the Ayrshire coast. We each selected a balloon and flew round to size up the problem before committing ourselves to opening fire. It was as well we did, for both were trailing long lengths of mooring wires beneath them, making it difficult to come up from below without becoming tangled with the ropes. My first burst seemed to have no effect at all; the wretched gasbag continued to float serenely on. The next time I dived steeply some distance from the target before pulling up vertically under it and letting fly with the Spitfire's eight Brownings. This time the envelope must have been punctured at the top, for the balloon began to lose shape, and gradually its altitude, as it continued to collapse. I called Glyn to advise him of the difficulties, but he had already discovered them for himself for, in the distance, the other aircraft could be seen pulling up directly below the second balloon. We rejoined formation and watched the two envelopes wriggling and spinning in wide circles before flopping into the sea off Arran. We landed to refuel before taking off again to help track down the elusive Commandos.

It was now late afternoon and we reckoned the attacking force must be well on its way if it was to have any hope of reaching the objective before nightfall. Thus I concentrated my search in the areas around Lochwinnoch Valley and Misty Law Moor. Back and forth I went, searching every roadway and hillock, but without any sight of the quarry. Groups of khaki-clad figures were here and there seen patrolling likely approaches or spread out along escarpments which gave them good all-round vantage points. Off Wemyss Bay the river steamer *Glen Sannox* was making her way southwards, the paddle wheels leaving a frothy trail in her wake and doubtless carrying a full complement of trippers on her weekend cruise to Ardrossan. Glaswegians are seldom slow to take advantage of an unexpected spell of good spring weather. I called up the General's Headquarters to find out how things were going and whether there had been any sightings.

'Negative, Villa Leader. Negative! No sightings reported so far. Suggest you patrol area Beta.'

This was becoming ridiculous. You just can't hide two hundred tough characters like that when the entire countryside is teeming with keen-eyed soldiery all intent on seeking them out. In any case they must be closing up by now in preparation for their final assault. A shortage of fuel dictated my return to base. The Adjutant met me on landing.

'The police have been on, Sir. Apparently they have had a complaint from some chap in Ugdale who is claiming that a hail of spent bullets rattled down on his roof and that he intends to sue the Air Ministry. The Inspector was wanting to know if any of our aircraft have been firing their guns this afternoon!'

'Ring up and tell them our friend in Kintyre can thank his lucky stars it was only spent bullets that came down around him. It could easily have been a ruddy great balloon! Tell the Inspector I will call at his station tomorrow morning to make out a report. I will have to stay around here until the exercise is finished. Is there any news of the Commandos yet?'

General Walker was becoming discouraged with the whole affair and, although too much of a gentleman to say so, was having little faith in our role as spotters. So was I for that matter, for we had put a great deal of effort into the affair – we had even augmented our force by the inclusion of the squadron's two-seater Magister trainer. I could not understand it.

The telephone rang shortly after five o'clock. It was the General on the line.

'You will find this hard to believe, Johnstone, but the

blighters are already *in* Ardrossan – every one of them!'

Crafty old Lister. He too had taken a fancy to the fine spell of weather and had decided to take his lads for a sail 'doon the watter' – all the way from the Broomielaw to Ardrossan. They had been on the *Glen Sannox* all the time!

13

UNLUCKY FOR SOME

Glyn Ritchie reminded me what day it was.

'Isn't it remarkable how often special things seem to happen to us on a thirteenth? I wonder what today will bring!'

Certainly the number thirteen had taken on a special significance in relation to 602 Squadron for, after all, had we not moved from Grangemouth to Drem on Friday, 13th October a year and a half ago – thirteen of us flying thirteen aircraft across, only to find that Drem at the time was No 13 Flying Training School and that we were operating under the control of No 13 Group, Fighter Command? Strangely too we had gone off to Dyce on 13th April and to Westhampnett on Friday, 13th August, while only a spell of very bad weather had prevented us from flying to our present location on 13th December. Yes, it was indeed remarkable. We would just have to wait and see what would turn up on this, the thirteenth day of March 1941.

Glyn had met me off the train from Glasgow, where I had been spending a couple of days in our flat where Margaret, my wife, was awaiting the arrival of our first-born. I had driven there in my aged Vauxhall and had put it into the Hyndland Garage for a much needed servicing and had come back by rail. In truth, the wretched vehicle was only fit for the scrap heap but, as I could still coax it along in fits and starts, had decided to keep it on the road a little while longer. In any case the car had only cost £30 when I had bought it third or fourth-hand in 1938 and there seemed little point in lashing out on another when it was so difficult to come by enough petrol to make it worth while.

Glyn parked his car outside the Orangefield Hotel and we walked through a gap in the hedge leading to the Old Mill. The Adjutant was in my office, where a heaped IN-tray had a daunting look about it. Clearly I was about to pay the penalty for taking two days off!

'I've left the training returns for your signature, Sir. Also Group Captain Rogers is flying up from Group to see you this morning. Apparently the Germans have laid a beam over Glasgow and Group wants us to take part in a "Fighter Night" this evening to be on the safe side. The Group Captain says he will take the returns back with him. Would you like a cup of tea, Sir?'

This was disturbing news. For some time the Germans had been working to perfect a navigational beam to guide bombers to their target areas and lately had been experimenting with a system of laying two beams together which intersected over the target itself. Of course, our backroom boys had not been slow to react to this piece of wizardry and Professor Jones and his team of boffins had already succeeded in 'bending' some of the German beams, much to the puzzlement of the Luftwaffe lads relying on them for help. Nevertheless, the possibility that they were laid in this direction boded ill for Clydeside. Forewarned is forearmed, but they had nevertheless caught us at a bad time, for with so many of our old hands posted elsewhere, 602 Squadron was now very short of night-trained pilots. In fact we had only four, including myself. Glyn Ritchie, Paul Webb and Roddy McDowall were the other three, but Paul was away on leave. However several squadrons were now re-equipped with twin-engined Beaufighter aircraft fitted with special radar detecting gear and were already making their presence felt in the South. One of these specialised night fighter units was based at Drem, but we were nevertheless very thinly defended in the air throughout Scotland as a whole.

In an effort to combat the heavy night attacks, another bright spark had recently come up with an idea for saturating a likely target with anti-aircraft defences – a scheme which appeared workable in principle but which had never been put to the test. His plan was to leave the lower air space entirely free of fighters and allot it for the anti-aircraft guns' attention – say from ground level to a height of 12,000 feet. Night fighters would then patrol at intervals of 500 feet from 14,000 feet upwards, leaving the intervening 2,000 feet clear for faulty shell fuses. It would call for accurate flying if collisions between the tightly packed fighters were to be avoided.

And so it appeared that the Group Captain Training was flying from Newcastle to discuss our participation in the first attempt at a 'Fighter Night', as the scheme was named, although our meagre contribution was unlikely to add much to its effectiveness. However that was not our fault, for I had long been at loggerheads with the personnel staff at Group Headquarters about the excessive numbers being posted away, and had pointed out that Group was rapidly denuding the effective strength of the squadron to such an extent that we were in danger of becoming nothing more than a non-operational training outfit. Indeed it was taking us all our time to get a few of the new boys into the air on Spitfires during favourable daylight conditions and none were anywhere near the stage of tackling a night sortie.

A black Beaufighter joined the circuit and swept out to sea preparatory to lining up for its final approach. A check call to the control tower confirmed it was Rogers, who was flying one of the night fighters, intending to take part in the forthcoming exercise with us. I went to the hardstanding to await his arrival.

The aircraft had not shown up five minutes later, but possibly the pilot had flown off to take a look at Arran. Ten minutes went by and still no sign of Group Captain Rogers. McDowall ran across the bridge towards me.

'There's an aircraft down in the sea off Troon. They think it's the Group Captain!'

We jumped into the staff car and made for the coastal road leading to Troon. About half a mile along it we came upon a police car and an ambulance drawn up at the side of the road, with a small group of people clustered round. Before reaching the spot however, we saw two stretchers being loaded into the ambulance which then drove off rapidly in the direction of Prestwick. A policeman wrapped in a blanket was on the point of getting into his car, his uniform saturated with sea water.

'I'm afraid the pilot has had it, Sir, but the other fellow has only been knocked out. They're taking them to the cottage hospital. Excuse me if I rush off, but I had to wade a long way out to reach them, and I'm soaked through.'

Not surprisingly the telephone had been red hot while we had been off the airfield and there was a message for me to ring the AOC as soon as I returned.

'This is a tragedy, Johnstone. I can't think what can have gone wrong, but I want you to find out. I am putting you in charge of the Court of Inquiry and would like you to start on it straight away. O'Neill will join you tomorrow. Perhaps you don't know, but that was Rogers' first trip in a Beaufighter and you might bear it in mind when you do your investigation. Also, in spite of what has just happened, we intend to go ahead with our "Fighter Night". The Guns have been alerted. How many crews can you raise?'

This was hardly the time to climb on my hobby-horse; doubtless the AOC was well aware of my misgivings and I merely replied that three was all we could muster. He thus ended the conversation with a curt 'Humph! – Well, do what you can!'

I was anxious to get inside the Beaufighter before anyone started playing around with the controls, for there could well be a simple explanation for the mishap. Nevertheless, by the time I had returned to the scene, ground crews had already secured a rope to the undercarriage and were hauling the wreckage ashore with the aid of a tractor borrowed from a local farmer. I would have to act fast.

The sea was bitterly cold and was up to my waist before I could get close enough to clamber into the aircraft. However the cockpit was clear of the water, which enabled me to make a thorough check of the positions of the various switches and cocks, just as they had been set before the aircraft hit the sea. One by one the more likely causes could be eliminated.

The tail trimmer was correctly set for a landing: The undercarriage was lowered and locked in the 'down' position: The rudder, elevator and aileron controls moved freely: The fuel cocks were – ah yes, let me see ...

Turning over the sodden pages of the Handling Notes, I found the section marked 'Control of Fuel Supply' in which was a paragraph drawing attention to a need to change over from one tank to another after one hour's flying. It would seem the Group Captain had missed this item, for subsequent investigation revealed that although the port tank had run dry, the other was full of petrol, and the engines must have cut out just as he was settling down for a landing. What rotten luck.

*

The crew room was buzzing with excitement that evening, for this was to be no exercise: It was the real thing.

Glyn, Roddy and I had been called to Standby and were already strapped into our cockpits waiting for the order to start engines and get airborne. We had been allocated patrol heights of 21,000, 20,500 and 20,000 feet respectively. Apparently the aircraft from Drem would be filling the lower slots. There had been no time for a rehearsal; the radar stations were already reporting large numbers of hostile aircraft approaching from the East and, in view of the pre-set beam over Clydeside, it was odds on they were heading for that area. We were none too happy about the immediate prospect either, for apart from going blindly into an operation we knew little about, we had loved ones living in the target area and were concerned for their safety. Besides, I was still shivering after my immersion that afternoon.

'All Villa aircraft – *scramble!*'

The Spitfires strained at the wheel chocks as the Merlins roared into life. A flarepath of paraffin goose-necks had been lit and we took off in quick succession before climbing at full throttle towards Glasgow. The night was dark and moonless, with patches of cloud scattered between eight and ten thousand feet. We had taken extra care when setting our altimeters before taking off, for it was going to be essential to maintain height accurately if we were to avoid colliding while circling the patrol point. A height separation of only five hundred feet was allowing very little margin for error in conditions such as these.

Settling in to the allotted station, I began to fly in a wide arc
to port. Fortunately a number of searchlight beams were
already probing the sky and the light bouncing off the clouds
was reflecting on the waters of the Clyde, so it was possible to
keep one's position. The controller's voice sounded strangely
remote as he intoned a running commentary on the raid's
progress.

'Three plus Bandits approaching Bellshill from the east at
Angels thirteen. Four plus over Grangemouth ...' and so on.

Flashes from bursting ack-ack shells flecked the sky to the
East, only faintly visible through the industrial haze.
Suddenly the guns immediately below opened up, when their
muzzle flashes were soon outshone by the brilliant explosions
of falling bombs. The enemy had arrived.

Our earphones became filled with a jumble of calls as one
pilot after another made a sighting.

'I see one. He's miles below!'

'There's another – Christ, can't I come down? ... Oh hell,
I've lost him!'

From the loftiness of 20,000 feet, I too caught occasional
glimpses of the unmistakable silhouettes of Heinkels far below
as they swept across the burning carpet, the rising smoke
suffusing the scene with a ghostly dark pink light.
Occasionally a particularly brilliant flash denoted another
large bomb or a land mine finding a target. It was like looking
into Dante's inferno as the flames took hold and spread along
the river bank, now clearly recognisable in the light from
burning buildings. But it would have been madness to have
deviated from the plan and come lower, as it would have only
jeopardised the others and possibly have led to the ultimate
disgrace of a court martial. So we continued to orbit the
ghastly scene, peering intently in all directions, hoping to pick
up one of the high flying bandits, but none came our way. We
had to remain the impotent, frustrated, spectators of a
holocaust unfolding beneath our very eyes.

And so we continued to patrol to the limit of the aircraft's
endurance before breaking off and returning to refuel. In no
time we were airborne again and heading back towards

Clydeside, whence the glow from the fires was visible as soon as we were off the ground. But it was another frustrating effort, for it was all over by the time we were back on patrol and, apart from a triumphant shout from one of the Beaufighter boys to say he had got one down near Turnberry, the ether was oddly silent. Everyone had gone home, including the Germans who had departed, leaving behind a massive calling card of flames and destruction.

But how had they got through so easily? That was the question which occupied the minds of many for days to come. The biggest doubt was whether it had been sheer coincidence alone that the bombers had all approached the target area at heights between 12,000 and 14,000 feet – the so-called 'safety zone' – or had someone been talking beforehand? Maybe the answer will never be known. Sufficient to say that the disaster effectively put paid to any further attempts to mount a 'Fighter Night'. It was just our bad luck that it should have been given its one and only airing over our own city.

*

No one said much as we paced the room waiting for the dawn to break. All communications with Glasgow had been put out of action and there was no means of finding out what had occurred there. From above it had appeared that the biggest fires were burning in the West End of the city or down the river towards Clydebank. If so, my wife was somewhere in the middle of it. The purgatory of that night only ended when the first streaks of light heralded a new day and we were permitted to come off duty.

No vehicle ever covered the ground in less time than my staff car as I drove pell-mell over the Fenwick Moor and into the southern outskirts of the city. Through Newton Mearns, Whitecraigs and into Pollokshaws Road, but still no sign of damage, although it crossed my mind that there were no tramcars, and very few other vehicles, on the streets. Then suddenly the way ahead was blocked with rubble from a fallen tenement building, amongst which many firemen, Auxiliaries and other helpers laboured to move huge blocks of sandstone in their frantic search for possible victims trapped beneath the stones. A group of onlookers stood idly by, the agony of the night etched grimly on their faces.

Across King George V Bridge, mercifully spared, through the city, making frequent diversions wherever the road ahead had not been cleared, and on into the West End, where scenes of devastation were growing ever more profuse as I neared Hyndland Road. Heart in mouth, I braced myself for the worst. But, thanks be to God, the tall red sandstone block of flats was still there, dingy as ever, apparently untouched. I belted up the three flights of stairs, taking them two at a time. Margaret greeted me as if nothing unusual had happened.

'I wondered if you might phone. We had some bombing last night. It was very noisy and the kitchen window blew in. It was really quite funny, though, for the blast turned on one of the kitchen taps and we were nearly flooded! Did you know there had been a raid?'

It was not only the effort of running up the stairs which left me speechless! This was one of the many occasions when I realised it was quite impossible to understand what makes the average woman tick. The sheer impudence of the question left me completely bereft of words. Did I know there had been a raid indeed! I just sat down and laughed – the relief at finding her unharmed was beyond measure.

The story unfolded bit by bit. Bombs had fallen nearby in the Botanic Gardens, Turnberry Road, Dudley Drive, Kelvingrove Park and Partick Station whilst a land mine had all but demolished the Hyndland Garage just round the corner. This had probably been the explosion which had damaged the kitchen window. In view of a certain vested interest therein, I wanted to inspect that myself. I had little doubt that I had seen the last of my Vauxhall.

The site was deserted. A high pile of rubble, contained by two walls still standing, was all that remained of the Hyndland Garage. Wrecks of cars protruded here and there from among the debris, together with remains of the roof girders now contorted into many grotesque shapes. Never mind, I had had my money's worth out of the old boneshaker! I went back to the flat and waited while Margaret packed her things, as I was taking her with me to Prestwick, where I could keep an eye on her while we waited for the baby to arrive.

Three days later I had a telephone call from the manager of the garage.

'When are you coming to collect your car, Mr Johnstone? We had done the servicing on it before we were hit. Yours was about the only one fit to drive away once we got to the bottom of the pile. There's a wee dent in the bonnet, but nothing that a touch of paint won't put right!'

The thirteenth, eh? Maybe special things do tend to happen whenever that number comes up, but happily they are not *always* unlucky things!

14

A MATTER OF URGENCY

Whichever way you read it, the signal from the Air Ministry was quite specific. It could only mean one thing – I was being posted overseas. To the Middle East in fact. Furthermore, I was wanted there in a hurry, for the signal said that too – 'Officer is to report to Headquarters, RAF Middle East a.s.p.'. That also could only mean one thing – As Soon As Possible! Of course other relevancies were mentioned, such as being medically examined and kitted out in accordance with some regulation or other. But the meat of the message was unmistakable – I was to go abroad.

As expected, my wife was none too pleased when I broke the news that evening, for we had only recently found rented accommodation in the outskirts of Edinburgh whilst I did a stint as a Fighter Controller at RAF Turnhouse. It had been the first attempt at setting up house since our marriage eighteen months before and our first-born was but four months old, Ann having first seen the light of day at Prestwick, whence I had moved Margaret for her own safety after the Germans had begun to direct their unwelcome attentions on Glasgow. That day in March had repercussions for me too, for I had developed such a chill after wading out to the crashed Beaufighter, that it developed into pneumonia and I had to be taken off flying. I was therefore doing a spell at the blunt end although, if the truth were known, I was quite enjoying the experience and therefore viewed the pending exodus with some disfavour.

The Station Adjutant handed me a bulky envelope.

'You will crease yourself with laughing when you read this, Sandy. Don't have a fit!'

Accompanying a sheaf of forms, instructions and other pieces of literature, both instructive and inquisitive, was a handbook entitled *Hints for Officers Proceeding Overseas for the First Time*. It was indeed a remarkable document, for in it I was informed that it was permissible to take up to ten hundredweights of baggage, to be packed, if possible, in wardrobe trunks: it was *essential* to take evening clothes in addition to both home and tropical weight mess dress: polo ponies could normally be procured less expensively abroad, although arrangements could be made to ship out the officers' own mounts if so desired: if a private car was being taken, the following licences would be required ...: a further licence to carry firearms had to be obtained before they could be taken out of the country. Turning back to the flyleaf, I discovered the book had been published in 1935! Now it was early September 1941 and the nation had been at war for two years.

I waited impatiently for instructions to tell me where to pick up an aircraft to fly to the Middle East, for undoubtedly that would be the quickest way to get there, and I was wanted in a hurry.

'You are to report to No 1 Personnel Despatch Centre next Monday. I think that is Padstow. I'll just check. No, not Padstow – Padgate, near Warrington. The Flight Sergeant will make out a railway warrant for you!'

I could have willingly wrung the Adjutant's neck, for Padgate was notorious as one of the RAF's forgotten outposts. It was dreary in the extreme.

'I thought they would have given me an aircraft to fly. Maybe I'll be sent on to an airfield when I get to Padgate.'

'The movement signal doesn't mention anything about flying. It says a sea passage has been arranged.'

*

The trauma of parting over, I arrived at No 1 PDC after nine miserable hours in an unheated, and uncatered-for, train which, as if to accentuate the pangs of parting, had actually steamed close by our little home as it pulled out of Edinburgh.

Ours was apparently the first draft of officers to be handled by this particular PDC, and I could well believe it. Irrespective of rank, all were accommodated together in a large barrack room containing twenty-four iron frame beds, on each of which lay a straw-filled palliasse. No blankets were provided, which necessitated seeking out our camping kit to find the required covering. However my neighbouring bedfellow, a young Sikh pilot officer, provided an interesting diversion next morning when he went through the ritual of 'preparing' his whiskers and struggled to wind up his puggaree. The rest of the day was taken up standing in a series of queues whilst arrival documents, posting documents, medical documents and various other documents were checked against our names. We were also issued with an astonishing khaki-coloured policeman's helmet – a solar topee, we were informed, which had always to be worn when out in the sun.

No one at Padgate had heard anything about an aircraft to be flown to the Middle East. Indeed, I began to wonder whether anyone there even knew what an aeroplane looked like. In any case, who had said anything about the Middle East? Our destination was supposed to be secret, didn't I know that?

It was dark before we lined up outside to be marched, kitbags on our shoulders, to a nearby railway halt where our 'Special' was to pick us up at midnight. Goodness knows from which museum the rolling stock had been taken, for the carriages were clearly pre-1914 vintage. Then, of course, corridors were unthought of, the seats were hard and upright, whilst the only illumination came from a small blue bulb stuck into the erstwhile gas-lamp fitting. Even the outside door handles were of the old brass carriage type.

Thus began a second miserable railway journey within the space of two days. The train jerked; it juddered; it shook; it stopped – interminably. None knew where we were headed, for the veil of secrecy had been maintained at Padgate right up to the time of our departure. However, in view of Padgate's proximity to the port of Liverpool, the latter seemed the most likely point of embarkation but, as hour succeeded uncomfortable hour, it became clear we were heading elsewhere. Juddering and jerking throughout the night, no one could identify the landscape when every now and again a blind was raised surreptitiously and a head poked out of the window. The route had us baffled.

Towards dawn we drew into a large station and ordered out to stretch our legs and to pick up a sandwich and a mug of tea provided off a trolley by a member of the Women's Voluntary Services. Apart from the dim light cast by a few masked lamps, the platform was in darkness. Could the angel of mercy please tell me where I was?

'Och, you're in Edinburgh – This is Waverley Station!'

Twenty minutes later I was again chuffing past our little home in the outskirts of the city which I had left only two days previously. It seemed like a decade!

But now it was daylight and I was in familiar territory. We were heading for Glasgow and should arrive at Queen's Street Station within the hour. Not a bit of it. Somehow the train managed to by-pass the centre of Glasgow altogether and eventually drew to a halt alongside an ocean going liner berthed in the King George V docks. HMT *Almanzora* was to be our floating home for the next few months.

*

The signal lamp was flashing from the bridge of *Strathaird*, aimed at the old French trooper *Mendoza*. It seemed the Commodore was once again exhorting her skipper to try to keep up, but to avoid making smoke while doing so. This was meant to be a 'twelve-knot' convoy but its progress was being hampered by the inclusion of the aged French liner, whose engines had seen better days and were obviously having difficulty in maintaining enough revs.

We had been at sea now for five days, having finally set sail after an interminable three days tied up at the dockside, followed by a further five anchored off the Tail o' the Bank, before slipping silently through the Gantocks Boom in the dead of night. Other ships from the Mersey joined the convoy off Northern Ireland and now it was a formidable armada which was steaming bravely into the Atlantic Ocean – forty-five ocean-going merchantmen with a sizeable escort of RN cruisers, destroyers, frigates and the aircraft carrier *Argus*. Three empty cross-channel steamers sailed alongside to pick up survivors in the event of any ships falling victim to the ever-prowling packs of U-boats lurking in the dark waters. It was cold and stormy and it had been far from comfortable so far. Even *Argus* was taking it 'green' over her flight deck and was unable to fly off any aircraft.

The veil of secrecy was being maintained. No, we could *not* be told where we were headed. Indeed, we began to wonder whether our Captain knew either, for the entire fleet altered course every five minutes or so as it zigged and zagged into the Atlantic. At least we thought it was the Atlantic before Johnny Revell stuck his astro-sextant through a porthole one night and pronounced gravely that we were somewhere north of Iceland. The stormy seas, added to the sub-zero temperatures, certainly lent credence to his navigational prowess. Indeed we also began to wonder whether the issue of tropical uniforms had been nothing more than a gigantic confidence trick designed to baffle the enemy, although our aged Colonel OC Troops still insisted we wore topees during the daily muster at the lifeboat stations.

Our escort of three Sunderland flying boats left on the third day, after which the only aircraft sighted had been a German four-engined reconnaissance Condor, which doubtless advised the hidden U-boats of our presence. It was an uncomfortable feeling and thenceforth the lads took the lifeboat drills much more seriously.

Inboard, however, we were comfortably berthed. *Almanzora* had only recently come off the regular Royal Mail run to South America and had not yet been converted to troopship standards. Consequently I found myself the sole occupant of a first class cabin. Also the bar still operated at reasonable prices and, when not parading with our topees, we were able to pass the time away pleasantly enough with games of shuffleboard, deck tennis, liar dice, poker or by browsing through books from the well-stocked ship's library. However, we missed the company of the ladies, for there were none on board our ship.

After a week at sea we noticed that some of the ships had disappeared from the columns and that the weather was beginning to improve. It transpired that part of the convoy had hived off and gone into Halifax and that we had come within one day's sailing of the Canadian coast. Johnny's sextant was again put to work when he came up this time with the information that the convoy was in mid-Atlantic and steering an easterly course. At two a.m. on the twentieth day out, the alarm bells had us tumbling from our bunks to muster at the lifeboat stations, clad in pyjamas, life jackets and topees, when members of the ship's staff went the rounds, enquiring from each of us in turn –

'Do you see those lights over there?'

Having assured them that we could indeed just make out a few lights in the distance, we were promptly dismissed and told to go back to bed, not unnaturally puzzled as to the reason for being thus disturbed in the middle of the night. The Captain put us wise next day over a pink gin.

'It's an old trick, that one! You see, the law permits homosexuality at sea after a ship has been out of sight of land for not less than twenty-one days. We altered course last night to come within sight of the Azores!'

Only he did not put it quite that way!

It was relief to make landfall at Freetown after scattering the ships to dodge a pack of U-boats waiting in their path. A number of Movements staff came on board, whom we assumed would arrange passages ashore, for we were all in need of a change of scenery.

'We are sorry you are not allowed off the ship. The local authorities won't permit it!'

The RAF member of the staff produced a list from a briefcase.

'Will the following please step forward. Arrangements have been made for some of you to be flown from here direct to Cairo.'

I waited eagerly for my name to be called. I must surely be on the list for, after all, I was wanted urgently in the Middle

East. My Posting Notice said so.

'No, I'm sorry. Your name is not on the list!'

Repeated entreaties, backed by the production of the Notice itself, failed to secure a place on a trans-African flight so, with the remainder, I had to suffer the equatorial heat of Freetown harbour for a further week, while the ships took on fresh supplies before heading into the South Atlantic and their next port of call. Crossing the Equator, we wondered vaguely whether the stokers in the engineroom were wearing their topees in case the sun should shine straight down the funnel!

It was the same reaction at Durban.

'Sorry, Sir. We have no instructions to fly you anywhere!'

But at least we met some women.

Nevertheless my destination was no nearer after six weeks' travelling and I was reluctantly coming to the conclusion that the posting instructions were not worth the paper they were printed on, so I might as well accept the inevitable and follow the teaching of Confucius to 'relax and enjoy it'!

Although continuing to zig and zag up the Indian Ocean, the convoy was no longer under threat as it steamed northwards. The battle cruiser *Repulse* had joined us at Durban and the sight of this mighty bulwark in our midst added to a spirit of wellbeing among the ship's company. Besides I was heading in the right direction at last.

It was with some emotion that we watched *Repulse* parting company when we reached Cape Gardafui ten days later. Little did anyone realise, as she steamed majestically at full speed through our lines, that this great vessel was sailing off to become the victim of Japanese bombers less than two months later.

Conditions became unbearable when we turned into the Gulf of Aden, for what little wind there was was dead astern and we were stifled for lack of air. The bulkheads became too hot to touch and, as none of the ships was fitted with any form of air conditioning, the Commodore was constrained to head the fleet into wind to pick up what little breeze remained. At least we were able to breathe again. Of course, having turned through one hundred and eighty degrees, *Mendoza* found herself way out in front for once. The signalman in *Strathaird* got busy on his lamp again.

'*Mendoza* ahoy, Bravo! *En avance au vent!*'

The convoy dispersed at Aden, for the port of Suez had been subjected to heavy bombing and it had been deemed prudent to allow only one ship at a time to berth there for unloading. Hence we steamed up the Red Sea on our own, having embarked at Aden an Arab sheik and his retinue who travelled with us as far as Port Sudan, where he was greeted by a multitude of followers waiting to welcome him. Little did they know that, during the voyage, their distinguished visitor had become 'one of us' in the bar, where he had shown a considerable aptitude for downing large pink gins! He was an engaging character whose full set of steel dentures only added to his unusual charm. Like *Repulse*, we were sorry to see him go.

When the anchor finally dropped at Port Taufiq, our disembarkation took place so quickly that none of us had time even to say farewell to the Captain and his officers who had looked after us so well during the long voyage. So this was Egypt, the land of the sand and the sun!

Sand, yes. There seemed to be nothing but sand. However, by the time we had hung around the docks all afternoon before a filthy three-ton lorry whisked us off to our sleeping quarters, it was dark. It appeared we had not been expected and, after driving some distance alongside the canal, the lorry turned into the desert for a few more miles before depositing its load at a tented camp, entirely surrounded by barbed wire. Only the absence of perimeter guards persuaded me we were not about to share the accommodation with a batch of Italian prisoners of war. The tents themselves had been pitched inside deep trenches dug out of the sand.

'It helps to keep out the cold!' we were informed. And cold it was. This was not my idea of the mystic East at all! I was becoming disillusioned.

Having eventually convinced the staff next morning that I was not part of Draft 116, whatever that was, and having flourished the Posting Notice at them for the umpteenth time, arrangements were made to transport me and my baggage to Headquarters, Middle East Air Force in Cairo. The Senior

Personnel Staff Officer looked up when I entered his office clutching the now well-worn, Posting Notice.

'I'm here, Sir!'

'I can see that – but who the hell are you, and what have you come here for?'

He took the Posting Notice and read it through.

'Never heard of you! No one told us you were coming. What were you doing before you left the UK?'

I explained I had been doing a spell as a fighter controller.

'Ah, fine. We're short of controllers. You had better go out to the Western Desert – they are for ever at me to send them more!'

My heart sank, for I had heard about conditions in the desert: Mobile Ops Rooms: scorching temperatures during the day and freezing at night: plagued by flies: hard rations: no water: no thanks! I turned to leave the room, already completely disillusioned with life in the Middle East. The SPSO called me back.

'By the way, Johnstone, do you speak French?'

For once my brain went into top gear.

'Fluently, Sir.'

'At that rate, you had better go to Beirut instead.'

Thank goodness I was not put to the test, for I could barely speak a single word of the language!

15

THE MILK RUN

It was no more than a silvery speck glittering in the cloudless sky, but the long condensation trail drew one's eye easily to its source. The aircraft was obviously flying very high.

'That's the second time the blighter has come over at this time of the week. It was midday last Thursday too, wasn't it? Let's hope Ken can get within reach of him today!'

Butch Barton shrugged his shoulders.

'I doubt it, Harry. I've never been able to get one of these crates above twenty-seven thousand and, besides, we need a lot more warning if we are to have any hope of getting within firing range.'

Barton turned to me.

'Have you any idea when we will get better radar out here, Sir? It seems we have been fobbed off with all the old stuff no one else wants!'

Butch's comment was not without substance. Since my arrival in Beirut two months earlier to help set up a co-ordinated fighter controlling system in the Levant, we had got about as far as was possible with the limited equipment at our disposal. Two mobile ground radar stations had been deployed, one at Tripoli in the north of the country and the other at Haifa, to give a measure of protection to the Palestine Sector. But their performance was woefully inadequate for the job in hand, and the enemy was apparently taking advantage of its shortcomings and had recently started flying regular reconnaissance missions over Beirut, presumably to keep an eye on what we were up to.

Our fighter strength was limited to the twelve Hurricanes of

451 Squadron, Royal Australian Air Force, which had arrived in the district to rest for a month after an arduous spell of fighting in the Western Desert. It was a large area for a single squadron to cover and we had been forced to deploy four aircraft to operate from the airport at Beirut, leaving the remainder to get on with it as best they could at a strip recently laid at El Bassa, immediately across the Palestinian border. El Bassa was an attractive place set among olive groves but, like Beirut, was lacking much of the sophisticated equipment required for instant fighter reaction. The same held true to a certain extent in the control room itself, where we had recently put the finishing touches to the makeshift centre, knocked up in the cellar of La Maison sur la Dune.

The two Hurricanes taxied to the dispersal. Ken Watts climbed down from his aircraft and gave us the thumbs down sign.

'We couldn't get within miles of him. He must have been at thirty thousand feet at least, and we couldn't even get close enough to have a shot at him. It was a Ju 88 though; we got near enough to see that!'

I looked at the four cannons protruding from the wings of the Hurricanes and at the strange protuberances of the sand filters fixed under their noses. The machines had a powerful look about them, but they were heavy, and the air filter must be having an adverse affect on the power output of their Merlin engines. I was pondering about this as I drove back to the Operations Room, for the seeds of an idea were beginning to germinate in my mind.

*

Heath Robinson would have been proud of the 'nerve centre' we had created in the Stygian gloom of the cellar in La Maison for, apart from linking together plots passed from the two radar stations, we had been able to augment this information by harnessing some of the local gendarmerie into a form of Observer Corps although, on account of the multi-national aspect of the force, we also had to employ a number of interpreters to unscramble their reports which came in in

French, Arabic, or even in some instances, Turkish. Nevertheless it was surprising how much information we were managing to glean from this source.

Of course there were other drawbacks to contend with for, apart from having to segregate the interpreters from the Ops Room proper because of security considerations, thus adding another link in the reporting chain, lengths of landline cable were mysteriously disappearing from outside the building. It was only when a culprit was caught red-handed one night, that we discovered the wire was being filched by itinerant Arabs who were using it to tie bundles to the backs of their donkeys. In a fit of pique at this wanton piece of sabotage, the Signals Officer had a notice erected, inscribed in five different languages, to the effect that anyone approaching within x yards of the notice was liable to be shot at. However, because the message was repeated five times, the lettering on the board was necessarily small, and those few Arabs capable of reading at all had to come right up to the sign to read what was on it, and so we continued to lose our lengths of wire!

The matter of blackout was another problem, for the Lebanese people, although most worthy and correct in their dealings with us, were patently uninterested in the progress of the war and it meant little to them that their erstwhile masters, the Vichy French, had been recently superseded by the British and the Free French, and they just wanted to be left to get on with their own lives. Also they had a strong antipathy to the thought of blacking out their homes at night for, they said, it was much too hot and stuffy when everything was closed up. So I called on the Mayor and was able to persuade him that it would be to everyone's benefit, including his own, if some form of blackout could be instituted, especially when we could give early warning of an approaching raider.

'You will never get the people to do it for themselves,' he told me. 'However you might be able to arrange with the operators at the central power station to switch off the electricity supply whenever there is a threat!'

And so a system of *'Alertes Jaunes'* and *'Alertes Rouges'* was agreed which would be phoned through to the power station at the appropriate moment. Indeed, we actually tested it once or twice and it worked satisfactorily.

The Deputy Chief of the Air Staff chose to visit Beirut a week later, when we were naturally eager to show off the operations set-up. We reckoned it was now working effectively within the limitations of the equipment and that nothing had been overlooked.

Sir Douglas and his ADC wiped their brows as they entered the cellar. It was very warm outside and they welcomed the relief afforded by the relative coolness below ground. I was in the midst of explaining to the distinguished visitor the various aspects of the system when a supervisor called from the floor.

'One Bandit approaching from the west, Sir. Range twenty five miles. Angels thirty plus. I think it's the Milk Run again.'

So DCAS would have an opportunity to see for himself how well we could do it!

Having scrambled two Hurricanes from El Bassa, we peered down at the plot, watching intently as the counters were moved across the table. A second plotting block showed the fighters' position as they climbed towards the intruder, although their height differential was considerable. However, I was pleased to notice that our visitors were impressed. Suddenly the Operations Room was plunged into darkness. I called out to the sergeant in charge.

'Get the lanterns lit – quickly!'

A stock of hurricane lamps was kept ready to cope with such emergencies, for we had not yet merited the luxury of our own generator. The sergeant could be heard scrabbling around as he fetched the lanterns and called for a box of matches, and we could see dimly the faces of the, now immobilised, plotters as he struck the first match. He let out an oath when it burned his fingers and the lantern refused to light. The globe of a second was removed, but it too failed to ignite. I despatched a runner to go outside to find out what was going on, but he soon returned to report that everything seemed to be in order and that he could actually see the raider overhead. The sergeant called for another box of matches.

By now our visitors were becoming restless and moved forward to obtain a better view of the table whenever a match was struck, but Sir Douglas, forgetting he was standing on a dais, stumbled against the plotting table and upset the box containing the plotting counters. In haste to assist his master, the aide cannoned into one of the supervisors and was sent sprawling across the table, thus demolishing the plot altogether. No one said anything; the only sound came from Sir Douglas, who merely grunted. A third box of matches was called for, but DCAS reckoned he had seen enough and we groped our way outside with some difficulty. The sun still shone brightly, but the raider had gone and a visit to the mess seemed timely.

I returned to the Operations Room as soon as the visitors departed, still hopping mad that we had been let down by such mundane items as a few lanterns. Damn it, I had checked every one personally to make sure they were filled with paraffin! By now the lights were on, our unimaginative friends at the power station having previously plunged us into darkness by interpreting our instructions literally, and pulling the plug immediately on receiving an *'Alerte Rouge'*. But, as they afterwards argued, no one had told them it only applied during the hours of darkness! A shamefaced NCO met me as I entered.

'There's no effing wicks in the lamps, Sir!'

*

The following Thursday saw me at the aerodrome, waiting for the call which would herald the arrival of the, now weekly, reconnaissance flight. I had been thinking over what to do to give the Hurricanes a better chance of coming to grips with the nuisance and had discussed my ideas with the squadron commander.

'Let's see what we can take off them to lighten the load. We could dispense with the armour plating for a start – and how about removing two of the cannons? Furthermore, on the assumption he will turn up on time, we need not carry a full load of fuel.'

And so two Hurricane 11C's had been stripped down and I intended to fly one myself on this occasion, for Herr Schmidt had been taking the mickey out of me for long enough. Ken Watts would fly as number two. It was very hot in the tent, but it was preferable to sitting in the cockpit in the torrid rays of the sun. The field telephone rang.

'Two aircraft of 451 Squadron – Scramble – One Bandit approaching from the West. Angels thirty plus.'

Ken and I were airborne within a minute and streaking over the sand dunes towards the sea. We knew which direction to steer without waiting for the controller to tell us, for we had seen enough of the intruder during the past month to have a pretty good idea of his flight path, and we had no reason to suspect he would deviate from it on this occasion. The ground fell away rapidly as the lightened Hurricanes bore upwards at full throttle.

'Bandit is twenty miles out at Angels thirty plus. Steer three-sixer-zero.'

Ahead, in the distance, we could make out the cloud-wrapped mountains of Cyprus whilst a glance in the mirror showed the town of Beirut falling fast astern. The two aircraft strained upwards – 15,000, 20,000, 25,000 feet – but I was still unable to spot the quarry: It was just our luck he was not making trails this day. Suddenly a momentary flash caught my eye as the sunlight caught his fuselage.

'Tally-ho, number two! Bandit at ten o'clock and above.'

The brief sound of a radio carrier wave told me that Ken had got the message. In such circumstances there was no need for chatter; a simple blip of the switch was all that was needed.

At 28,000 feet the Hurricane was becoming very sluggish on the controls and hard to handle. It had to be nursed, foot by foot, to gain more height. The sound of my heavy breathing came through the earphones as I sucked greedily at the oxygen.

'How are you making out, number two?'

'Struggling a bit. How about you?'

'The same, I fear. But keep going. We'll catch the blighter yet!'

At 30,000 feet the Ju 88 was still some two thousand feet above. Ken had fallen some way behind and was having difficulty in maintaining height as I turned gingerly to position below the intruder, the two black crosses now clearly discernible on the undersides of its wings. Switching on the gunsight and turning the ring to the 'fire' position I slowly – ever so slowly – eased back on the control column to aim a hundred yards in front of the target to allow for deflection. I pressed the firing button.

The cannons spat out their lethal loads, but the recoil proved too much for the old Hurricane, for it immediately lost all semblance of airworthiness and dropped a wing before turning over violently into an inverted spin straight towards the sea. Recovering at 25,000 feet, I found Ken was nowhere to be seen, but the Ju 88 was still in sight, streaking for home in the opposite direction to that in which it had arrived. There was clearly no point in giving chase and I called my colleague to pack it in and return to base.

The lads were eager to find out how we had got on.

'How near did you get? Any luck?'

'At least we got near enough to chuck something at him this time, but I don't think I hit him. Probably gave him a bit of a fright, though!'

I must have done. He never came back!

16

THE DORCHESTER

'Well, what do you think of it? Let's take a look inside.'

The massive concrete structure looked singularly out of place surrounded by three towering sides of the stone quarry in which it had been built. It reminded one vaguely of an ancient temple excavated from the deserts of Jordan, but it somehow did not look quite right there, nestling on the side of Mount Carmel. However I had brought it on myself and could do no more than sing its praises to its architect and builder, Colonel Bonn.

'It's jolly good, Bertie. Many thanks indeed. I'll be glad to get the Ops Room out of its present location, I can tell you. It's been worrying me for ages.'

A minor miracle had occurred at the turn of the year when I was promoted to the rank of Wing Commander with effect from 1st January 1942. Of course, this meant that I had to be found a job appropriate to the rank and so I was translated in April from the Ops post at Beirut to become the Sector Commander in Haifa. The change was equally to my liking.

The headquarters comprised a number of smart villas situated on the upper slopes of Mount Carmel, whilst the operations set-up itself was housed in one of the out-buildings of the nearby monastery. This particular retreat was considered unique in that it occupied the best site of all, being perched on the edge of the promontory overlooking the town of Haifa and the wide bay beyond. However, it was very vulnerable to attack from both the air and sea and we reckoned it could even be clobbered by a submarine, if one chose to surface close inshore and let fly with its guns. And so I had enlisted the aid of the Royal Engineers, whose commander had come up with plans to erect a reinforced concrete structure in a nearby disused quarry. It was the end product we were now discussing.

'There's only one thing, Bertie. Will it not be very easy to pick out from the air? All this white concrete must make it an obvious target.'

'How about taking me over the thing and I'll see whether it needs touching up?'

Bertie and I flew over the spot in a Magister.

'Crikey! It sticks out like a sore thumb, doesn't it? Never mind, just leave it to me!'

Two days later I was nearly blasted off my office chair when a loud explosion rocked the building, and my first thought was that the Coastal Defences' stock of ammunition had blown up. A column of smoke and dust rising into the air led me to the quarry, where a group was standing by the side of the road, gazing at the scene. Bertie saw me arrive.

'How about that, then? We'll take another look at it from the air, but I think it will be all right now!'

I stood amazed. The fine building had all but disappeared and only its entrance was now visible where it protruded from a pile of shattered rocks. The Colonel had blasted away the sides of the quarry so that the rubble had fallen on top of the new building, and I had no need to go flying to see that it would now be difficult to spot from above.

When I returned to the office, a signal was on my desk, telling me to report for interview with the Senior Air Staff Officer at Headquarters, Middle East the following day. However, it gave no indication of the reason for my summons to Cairo.

*

I felt like a naughty schoolboy standing in front of the Head as the Air Vice Marshal's steely eyes glared at me over the top of his half-moon spectacles.

'What's this you've done, Johnstone? An Ops Room, you say – well, who told you you could build it?'

I stammered that it was understood the project had been approved by Air Headquarters, Levant.

'Well, it hasn't! Have you got £85,000 to pay for it? No? Well, you had better come and see the Chief.'

The C-in-C's eyes were twinkling as I explained how the Operations Room had come about. Sir Arthur Tedder was not a man given to sudden outbursts of temper and, as the interview progressed, I gained the impression that he even had some sympathy for my uncomfortable predicament.

'It's fairly quiet here at the moment, so we'll fly up to Haifa together and I can see it for myself. Be at Helio for a ten o'clock take-off tomorrow morning.'

So, with Tedder at the controls, we took off from Heliopolis in a Mitchell bomber and touched down an hour later at St Jean d'Acre whence we were whisked off in a staff car at alarming speed, preceded by a twelve-strong escort of police outriders mounted on high-powered motor cycles. It was not every day the Commander-in-Chief visited these outposts! Now we were standing outside the new operations centre on the heights of Mount Carmel. Sir Arthur gazed at the edifice for some time before speaking.

'My God, what's this? The Dorchester?'

*

Surprisingly, the C-in-C's visit had been a success for, once recovering from the initial shock of seeing it for the first time, Sir Arthur warmed to the project and gave the building his formal blessing. Later, in the course of a convivial lunch, I mentioned to him how much I missed being at the sharp end and that it was now two years since I had held a flying appointment. Therefore his prompt reaction came as a pleasant surprise for, at best, I had not expected him to do more than pass on my remarks to his personnel staff, and I also knew that flying jobs for Wing Commanders were hard to come by in this theatre of operations. His letter nearly bowled me over.

Halifax which crashed
the WAAF site at
rwood Common

mbug Master' with his
rsonalised' Spitfire

utenant Helmberger
veys his Liberator –
rwood Common

A Mosquito six

Bently Priory

View of Bently Priory in
1944 showing the
'puddle-jumper' strip

I was to be given command of one of the fighter wings in Malta, the letter read. However, transportation to the island was difficult, but he had advised his people to put my name on the waiting list and hoped I would not be kept hanging around too long. A relief would be posted to Haifa within the next few days, after which I was to proceed to Cairo to await further instructions. In the meantime the matter of the Operations Room had been settled and he was sure the Dorchester would serve a useful purpose in years to come. Besides, the letter went on, I would doubtless be very welcome in Malta, where there was plenty of scope for a builder of talent, as the enemy had a nasty habit of knocking down every structure as soon as it had been put up!

There were worse places than Cairo in which to while away time awaiting transport to the beleagured island. Very few aircraft were making the journey, it seemed, for apart from a critical shortage of foodstuffs, the island had barely sufficient stocks of petrol to keep the defending fighters in the air, and none could be spared to refuel visiting aircraft for a return journey. Thus aircraft which ventured to Malta had to carry enough fuel for the double journey, with the result that their payloads were greatly reduced. Only essential personnel and supplies were being taken and there was a considerable backlog of personnel waiting to be ferried. I confirmed that my name had been added to the list, after which I could do no more than wait my turn.

With the Eighth Army pinned down at El Alamein and the entire coastline of Europe in enemy hands, Malta was indeed isolated from her friends. In fact, it was a miracle the island was holding out for so long and, as I continued to savour the fleshpots of the Egyptian capital, I could not help having a few qualms about my new posting, even if it did mean getting into the air again. The gallant defenders were fighting with their backs to the wall and even the Royal Navy had more or less given up using the place, as its erstwhile anchorage was no longer a haven of protection. Only an occasional submarine made the passage nowadays, and I would have travelled by that means if a berth had been available. However, discreet enquiries evoked the information that it was unlikely another sub would be heading that way from Egypt for at least another month. And so I stuck it out at Heliopolis awaiting a passage by air. When it came, its manner was unexpected.

'The Senior Accountant Officer has gone down with a bout of malaria, Johnstone. He should have been taking an important package to the island this afternoon and the AOA wants you to deliver it instead. Can you be ready to leave at four? There's an RAF Liberator going off then and we can squeeze you into it. Here's the package. Now, whatever you do, don't let it out of your sight – there's sixty thousand quid's worth of Maltese bank notes in it. Apparently the Malts are running short. Please sign this receipt!'

The Wing Commander handed over a bulky envelope, sealed with wax, and departed as soon as I had signed the slip. Enquiries confirmed that a Liberator was due to take off for Malta that afternoon.

The starboard engines were already running when I climbed into the bulky bomber and eased my way forward past countless bales and sacks containing dehydrated potatoes and, of all things, wellington boots. The wireless operator pointed into the bomb bay where a single naval torpedo glinted menacingly. It seemed to fill the entire area.

'I'm afraid you will have to travel down there, Sir. It's the only space left. However, I've left a couple of blankets for you to sit on. I hope you won't be too cold!'

I had not realised I was to have company on the trip until the entrance door opened again to admit an Army officer clutching a bulging briefcase and a bundle of newspapers. General Beckett shouted his introductions over the roar of the engines as the pilot ran them up, one after the other, to test the magneto switches. We sat facing one another, the torpedo cold against our knees, as we felt the aircraft trundling towards the end of the runway. We were on our way.

Darkness was falling by the time I had crawled out of the bomb well and made my way to the flight deck. The Nile Delta stretched its watery fingers outwards as we flew over the coast and out into the Mediterranean. The captain, a young Flight Lieutenant, pulled back one of his earpieces and shouted to me.

'I'm afraid I must ask you to stay in the bomb bay, Sir, in case we have a brush with enemy fighters. If we do, clip on your parachutes and hope for the best. If the worst happens, I will open the bomb doors and you will fall out with the torpedo!'

He laughed.

I returned to the well and passed on this cheering message to the General who was already shivering. The draught was whistling through the cracks in the bomb doors and it was not long before the steel casing of the torpedo felt like a block of ice. I offered my blanket to my companion, but he declined, not that it gave much protection against the arctic conditions in any case. The din from the engines, added to that of the wind whistling through the bomb bay, made conversation difficult, although we did our best.

'I've been over for a conference at GHQ,' he shouted. 'Been there for ten days. I'm CRA on the island. What are you going there for?'

I shouted back that I was supposed to be taking over one of the Spitfire Wings, but that the position might have changed when I got there, owing to the long delay while waiting for a passage. The General nodded to indicate he understood. I did not like to show my ignorance by inquiring what was a CRA. It was only later I discovered in what distinguished company I had been travelling, albeit very uncomfortably, in the bomb bay of a Liberator bomber. Joe Beckett was Commander, Royal Artillery – responsible for all anti-aircraft defences on the island!

The beam of a torch heralded the arrival of the wireless operator bearing two mugs of steaming cocoa and a couple of sticky buns. By now anything was a welcome relief after three and a half hours cooped up in the freezing misery of our confined quarters.

'We should be there in another hour,' he shouted above the noise of the engines.

The General asked him if he could borrow a torch as he had some papers he wanted to look at. The figure disappeared and returned with a heavy-duty torch which was handed down.

'Ah, that's better!'

The General fumbled inside his briefcase for the papers he was seeking, the light casting eerie shadows on the ribbing of the fuselage. Before struggling to ease out the correct document he removed a full bottle of Gordon's Gin from the overfilled case, but replaced it as soon as he found what he had been seeking. At that point, I confess he went down in my estimation, for I had momentary hopes of something a little stronger with which to pep up the cocoa. The General saw the look on my face.

'Sorry, old boy, it's not what you think it is. It's only holy water! The bishop asked me to bring some back with me and this empty bottle was the only thing handy when I was near the Jordan! I damned nearly forgot to bring it too!'

Not to be outdone, I showed my package.

'This is no good to us either, General!'

We had been airborne over four hours when the aircraft banked steeply and we heard the scuffle of feet as the crew members hurried back to action stations. The General and I clipped on our parachute packs, completely in the dark as to what was going on upstairs. We continued to circle.

'It can't be fighters, Sir. We would not be going round in circles if it was. Let's nip up and take a look.'

It took us some time to extricate ourselves from the bay; our limbs were cramped and stiff after so many hours confinement in our ice chest. We edged our way forward.

'Christ! Just look at that! These are my boys, don't y'know.'

About ten miles ahead was a scene reminiscent of a Brock's benefit. The sky twinkled with flashes from bursting shells whilst, below, more brilliant sheets of flame betokened bombs exploding on the ground. Malta was being subjected to one of its frequent poundings and our aircraft had been ordered to stand off until the raid was over and we were thus being treated to a grandstand view of it from the comparative safety of our circling bomber. Eventually all was darkness over the island when we were instructed to land and be turned round as quickly as possible, as the aircraft was to return to Egypt forthwith. The return payload would consist of Maltese civilians who were being compulsorily evacuated on orders from the Governor. There was not enough food for anyone on the island whose presence was not considered absolutely essential.

As soon as the aircraft came to a halt, several soldiers clambered on board and began to unload the cargo. It was apparent that the arrival of a few sacks of dehydrated potatoes was of considerably more significance than the return of their CRA! We found our way outside, when the warm air hit us as if someone had opened an oven door in our faces, but it was a relief to be on solid ground again and be able to stretch our limbs. Suddenly a voice called my name out of the darkness.

'Are you there, Sandy? Here – over here! Come quickly. They're coming back, and put on your tin hat, for God's sake!'

Frank Tyson grabbed my arm and hustled me from the aircraft towards one of the aircraft blast pens. Anti-aircraft guns opened up all round us as fresh waves of German bombers rumbled overhead.

'We haven't a hope of reaching a shelter. This will have to do. Shield your face with your arms. Nice to see you again, old man. What have you been doing with yourself since we last met?'

Frank had been the regular Adjutant of the Edinburgh Auxiliary squadron prior to the war, and we had not seen each other since. We had much to talk about, but sensible conversation had to cease when the bombs started to fall around us.

Crump. Crump. Whee ... crump. The noise was deafening and the ground shook when we were straddled by a stick of bombs. I glanced quickly over my shoulder as one fell close to where we crouched against the wall and was just in time to watch it demolish a nearby stone building.

As a shower of stones and other debris cascaded around us, my thoughts turned momentarily to Bertie Bonn. This would have been just up his street!

17

THE STAFF OF LIFE

Frank's head and shoulders appeared over the top of the stone parapet as he grasped the iron supports to swing himself into the well of the tower. He clapped his hands together to rid them of the particles of rust.

'I'm sorry to be late, but I had to bring Timber's bread out to him. The silly ass is landing back at Takali and forgot to take it. Anything happening?'

'No. It's all quiet at the moment. Where have you left the car? I'll just pop over to the mess and have something to eat. I suppose it's the same old mixture as before?'

The sound of engines starting up drew our attention to the far end of the airfield where the aircraft of 145 Squadron had been positioned earlier that morning. A few minutes later ten Spitfires roared down the runway and flew off in a climbing turn towards the north. Frank twirled the little handle of the field telephone several times, but nobody answered. He rang again, but before he could get through to the Operations Room, a string of Me 109's suddenly appeared from behind the hill at Imtarfa and streaked towards us, their bombs slung menacingly underneath. Frank and I ducked behind the parapet as the first aircraft roared close overhead and released its bomb, which hurtled onwards to burst with a loud explosion immediately beyond the runway. Then the next aircraft, and the next, whilst the noise rose to a crescendo as fifteen 109's screamed overhead in succession and released their loads. We peered over the low wall of the tower, noting carefully where each bomb fell. The telephone rang.

'G Shelter. You had better take cover!'

'You're telling us!' replied Frank, holding the handpiece over the edge of the parapet.

'Sorry we were late with the warning, old fruit. They came in low and we didn't see them until the last moment!'

There was nothing more to be said. We just hoped the Controller appreciated our efforts to provide him with a live broadcast of the raid!

It was all over in a flash and a stillness settled over the airfield as the last raider swung westward to disappear behind the rising ground. In the distance we could see our Spitfires swooping down to intercept the 109's as they crossed the coast. In the meantime we had work to do.

I had started up the engine of the little Ford by the time Frank had descended the iron ladder, inwardly thanking Providence that the building had again escaped damage. He jumped in beside me and leant over the seat to pick up a handful of small red flags lying in the back of the car while we were speeding towards the far end of the runway. The first of a string of lorries was already approaching as Frank got out to place a flag alongside the largest crater scarring the landing area. We repeated the performance along its entire length until all eight craters on the runway had been flagged in this way, but we ignored those unlikely to affect the landings.

'Where the hell has Annie got to? Oh, here she comes!'

An aged steamroller clanked and hissed its way towards the runway, the engineer winding vigorously on the steering gear to aim his charge at the nearest crater into which one of the lorries had already tipped its load. Frank and I stood some way off while the remaining holes were filled in before returning to the tower to inform Operations that all was now in order for the fighters to come in. Only twenty minutes had elapsed since the last bomb had fallen.

The fleet of lorries drove off to reload whilst Annie chuffed off triumphantly to her protective shelter to await her next summons. We held Annie in high esteem, for she was unique – quite unique, as a matter of fact, for she was the only steamroller on the island still working and, touch wood, she seemed to be bearing a charmed life for, apart from a few dents on her boiler inflicted by falling stones, she had so far survived all the raids and was continuing to lend her invaluable weight towards keeping the runway at Luqa in usable condition.

Having told Frank I would collect the flags on my way to the mess, I had hardly time to sling a leg over the parapet before another loud explosion directed our attention to a delayed action bomb going off beside the runway. We looked at one another.

'My God! That was a close shave. Annie drove over that spot only a few minutes ago!'

Strange as it may be, this had become part of my normal routine since being posted as one of the Deputy Station Commanders at RAF Luqa. Not unexpectedly, my delayed arrival in Malta had jeopardised the opportunity of becoming a Wing Leader straight away. The AOC had been sympathetic but explained that the fellow he had appointed in my absence was doing very well and it seemed only right that he should be given his head. In any case, he promised me the next Wing that came up. However, the news neither surprised nor upset me, for I would thus have more time to become acclimatised to the conditions and be able to get in some useful practice flying before taking over my own unit. In the meantime I had joined Frank Tyson at the airfield.

The runway at Luqa was the only one on the island capable of taking large aircraft and, as we were entirely dependent on air supply to survive, it was essential to keep it serviceable at all times. Hence a fleet of lorries, loaded with in-fill material, always stood by to rush immediately to the runway after every raid to repair the bomb damage. Time was of the essence, as the job had also to be completed quickly enough to recover our own fighters and, in order to ensure repairs were made in the correct sequence, Frank and I would take it in turn to sit on top of the only structure of any consequence still standing on the aerodrome, to plot the fall of the bombs. I thought the designation 'G Shelter' had been a masochistic misnomer until finding out that the tower also served as a ventilator shaft for a deep air raid shelter below. However, after living for several weeks with bombs whistling past my ears two or three times a day, I was looking forward to the moment when a Wing Leader's job would become vacant and I could swop the lofty perch for the comparative safety of a Spitfire's cockpit.

I had another reason, too, for wanting to join the flying elite. Food – or rather the lack of it, for the normal daily ration was, to say the least, meagre. Soups and stews, occasionally augmented with reconstituted potatoes, were the order of the day, the latter usually comprising a gravy of sorts in which floated lumps of goat's meat. We had our suspicions that a certain amount of dog flesh also found its way into the pot whenever supplies of the latter ran out. Inevitably anything heated had large blobs of oily soot floating on it, as the only means of cooking was over open burners stoked with fuel taken out of crashed aircraft. The rapidly diminishing stock of coal and coke on the island had to be reserved for the power station and hospitals, although a small amount was set aside for Annie's exclusive use. Added to this meagre diet we were each given a thick slice of bread every morning, and woe betide anyone who tried to snaffle more than his fair share. In consequence, everyone took to carrying around their daily bread ration with them, even stowing it in their aircraft when flying, in case they had to be diverted to another airfield. However a few eggs occasionally arrived in Malta from the neighbouring island of Gozo, but these were always earmarked for the aircrews. Hence my added impatience to get back on flying.

*

The worst of the blitz was over by the end of 1942 and there was no longer a need for two Wing Commanders to remain at Luqa. So, as none of the Wing Leader posts had yet become vacant, I had been transferred to the Fighter Operations Control Centre situated in a deep shelter beneath the Joint Headquarters in Valletta, where my previous experience as a controller could be put to some use. But today something out of the ordinary was taking place in 'The Ditch'.

Coming on watch at midday I found Dusty Miller, the Chief Controller, deep in conversation with a group of strangers, some who wore earphones, whilst others were leaning over the rail with Roger Frankland, who was explaining something of the plotting procedures on the large table below. Dusty signalled me to come over.

'Sandy, come and meet the BBC. They're here to make a recording of a typical scene in the Malta Fighter Operations Centre at the height of the battle and they want plenty of action. Have a word with Roger about a part in it for yourself. We're just about to begin.'

I took my place on the dais alongside Roger. The BBC team had set up two microphones in front of us, with others placed at strategic points throughout the centre, whilst a couple of large recording machines had been installed in a nearby office. The programme director rushed about making last minute adjustments, his earphones and script-board lending a professional air to the proceedings. This was going to be interesting, for I had never · before watched an outside broadcast team at work. Finally satisfied that all was in order, he raised an arm to signal the start of the programme.

Everything was quiet as the seconds ticked by. The director glanced querulously towards Dusty. The recording spools turned slowly on the machines. A minute passed. No one said anything. One of the sound engineers looked out of the office and made a despairing gesture towards the director. Still no sound.

Then Roger spoke.

'Three no trumps!'

It is for the record that the second run through was a little more informative!

*

When first announced, the news that a number of Spitfires were to be modified to carry bombs was greeted with considerable hilarity by the fellows.

'Corblimey! What can we do with a couple of two hundred and fifty pounders? I can't imagine them doing much damage unless, of course, we can drop them plumb on old Jerry's nut!'

But it was a fact. Since the enemy began to let up on his

concentrated attacks on the island towards the end of November, it had been possible for a few merchant ships to reach Malta unmolested and our stocks of fuel and ammunition were building up and, indeed, by the end of December we were encountering nothing worse than a few desultory raids by small formations of German fighters. We had not seen an Italian aircraft for ages and could only assume that either they had had enough or were being forced to divert their effort in support of Rommel's troops who were then in headlong retreat across the North coast of Africa. In fact the lads had become bored and it had been decided to carry the war into enemy territory for a change. Hence the belated introduction of the Spitfire Bomber, although the Germans had been carrying bombs under their 109's since the last quarter of 1940.

The AOC had detailed Tommy Thomson to devise a suitable method of aiming the bombs, for he realised it was not going to be easy, particularly as none of the converted Spitfires would be fitted with a bombsight. The long nose of the aircraft made it impossible for pilots to keep the target in sight once it had disappeared beneath it, and it would have been impractical to suggest they should stand up and lean over the sides of their cockpits! Through trial and error, however, Tommy decided that the best results were to be achieved by flying to one side of the target until it was level with the cockpit, then to roll the aeroplane over and dive straight downwards. Nevertheless the aircraft reached very high speeds during the vertical descent and, in the course of an early trial, one of the pilots pulled so much g-force during the recovery phase that the seat mountings collapsed, and the wretched fellow had to fly back to base more or less standing on one leg. However few live targets had been attacked, for supplies of the right bombs had not yet reached the island. When they did, however, we were in for a surprise, for they turned out to be five hundred pounders, fitted with percussion rods to make them explode three feet above the ground. This device made up in blast effect what the bombs lost in weight, but they were lethal by any standards.

The day came for me to set off on my first bombing mission.

Tommy, Nipple Heppel and I were to test the new weapons on a target in the nearby enemy-held island of Lampedusa. Fortunately I had been able to scrounge several trips in Spitfires beforehand and reckoned I had mastered the technique of bomb-aiming sufficiently to be trusted with a live weapon. Lampedusa had been chosen as the target for the island rarely had any fighter aircraft based on it, and its ack-ack defences were light and had never done more than lend an air of realism to the proceedings. In fact, Tommy had come to regard the place as a form of practice bombing range during his earlier tests.

Lampedusa could be seen in the distance soon after we reached operating height and it was not long before Tommy had us strung out in echelon formation, with myself in the outside position. I kept station on the other two Spitfires as they rose and fell on my starboard quarter, their bombs secured under the wings, with the lethal rods protruding beyond their leading edges. Tommy's voice crackled over the radio.

'Going down. Going down – *now!*'

Our aiming point was a group of stone buildings situated beyond the small landing strip which, our Intelligence people had informed us, housed the administrative services of the island. The target was coming abreast of me now.

Upside down: throttle closed: stick hard back: the altimeter unwinding like a clock gone crazy: the ground rushing up to meet me: sudden bursts of smoke as earlier bombs exploded round the target: the buildings dead centre on the gunsight: I pressed the button.

The Spitfire jerked upwards as the bombs fell away, but I had to exert considerable pressure on the control column to ease her out of the dive. As soon as we levelled off, I opened the throttle to chase after the other two whom I could see flying some distance ahead and above me. However there was something trailing beneath Heppel's aircraft which, on closer inspection, turned out to be one of the bombs which had failed to detach itself from its mounting. It was dangling, nose downwards, from the starboard wing of the Spitfire. Tommy had also spotted the problem.

'Red Two. Red Two. You have a hang-up. Can you jettison it?'

In spite of putting the Spitfire into a series of dives, followed by a sharp pull-up, Nipple was unable to shake the bomb loose. It refused to budge and continued to dangle, suspended from the rear toggle. Here, indeed, was a predicament, for the bomb was armed to go off on contact and it would be impossible to land the aircraft before the percussion rod first struck the ground. Thus we continued towards the coast of Malta, Nipple doing his best to rid his aircraft of its unwelcome appendage, whilst Tommy alerted the Controller of the problem.

'If the bomb won't come free, the pilot is to abandon his aircraft. Is this understood? He is to bale out. A rescue launch is on its way and will station off Halfar. It should be with you within the next fifteen minutes. Good luck!'

Soon the creamy wake of an Air/Sea rescue launch could be seen.as the powerful vessel swept clear of the Grand Harbour at nearly forty knots. The stricken aircraft continued to perform all manner of contortions whilst we flew nearby offering encouragement and advice to its pilot. But it was of no avail. Our fuel supply was running low when Heppel's voice, edged with anxiety, came over the radio.

'Red One. I'm about to bale out. Sorry about this!'

We watched, silent, as the Spitfire rolled on its back and the hapless pilot dropped out to hurtle, head over heels, towards the sea. After what seemed an eternity, the parachute started to stream and the canopy deployed, leaving Nipple swinging at the end of its cords like the pendulum of an old grandfather clock.

In the meantime the abandoned Spitfire had somehow righted itself and was now in hot pursuit of its pilot, as if incensed at being abandoned in such cavalier fashion. Round and round it flew, coming ever closer to the luckless Heppel hanging at the end of his parachute. Nipple said afterwards that, during one thrust, the Spitfire came close enough to make the canopy billow in the slipstream, when he thought his number was surely up.

On deck, the crew of the launch meanwhile watched

anxiously as the unmanned aircraft continued to wheel and cavort towards the sea, and no matter in which direction he swung the helm, the skipper was sure the Spitfire was aiming straight at his launch. As it happened, the AOA had that day chosen to show off the launch to his charming lady secretary and thus they had become unwilling participants in the unusual voyage. Indeed, they were being subjected to a great deal of buffeting as the boat was swung violently from one side to the other in its efforts to dodge the falling fighter. Nellie was not enjoying the experience one little bit!

However, as if tiring of its cat and mouse chase, the Spitfire finally gave it up and dived vertically into the sea a few cable lengths away, when the bomb blew up, sending a miniature tidal wave crashing down on the deck of the launch. Nipple was fished out of the sea, unharmed, five minutes later. Nellie swore she would never set foot on a boat again!

*

Our empty plates had been pushed to one side. We had been served corned beef for dinner that evening. Things were certainly looking up! Frank asked Nipple how he felt after his unfortunate experience.

'Hungry. Damned hungry! Can anyone let me have a piece of bread? I had mine with me in the aircraft!'

18

OFFENSIVE CAPERS

As the two Spitfires cleared the tip of Gozo Island and let down to sea level, I glanced right to make sure Tommy was still with me. However I need not have worried, for Tommy Smart knew all the tricks and was flying serenely along a hundred yards away. Indeed, he knew as well as I did that the success of the mission depended on our keeping below enemy radar cover until the last possible moment.

Another glance, this time in the rear-view mirror, showed the island receding rapidly astern whilst ahead to the north, I could already make out the irregular outline of the Sicilian cliffs in the distance. Above, numerous cotton wool clouds cast their shadows on the emerald sea below, here and there flecked with small white horses whipped up by the seasonal Mediterranean breezes. I could also see clearly the larger shadows of our aircraft as we skimmed low over the water. So far, so good.

*

Some distance inland, Giuseppe was roundly cursing his engine as he studied the gauges.

'*Mama mia!*' he expostulated to his fireman. 'Look atta da pressure! Itsa not enough hot. Itsa no good wood fire! Antonio, putta da more logs on – prontissimo!'

Giuseppe wiped his brow with a soiled piece of cotton waste whilst his colleague turned to do his bidding. Returning with an armful of roughly hewn logs, Antonio threw them into the firebox and leaned out over the side of the cab to make sure all the carriages were still attached, for he had known couplings to break before now and did not want his old friend Giuseppe to have to face the derisive banter of his workmates if he again turned up with half his train missing. However, everything was in order. The soldiers in the leading flat truck sat huddled round the flak gun, their backs to the engine to avoid smuts from the smokestack getting into their eyes. Some flicked at their grey tunics to rid them of the nuisance whilst others sat disconsolately, supporting their heads in cupped hands. Beyond, Antonio could see faces peering from open windows further down the train and smiled to himself at the knowledge that they were nearing the Palonia cutting, with half a mile of tunnel at its centre.

'Huh!' he remarked to his friend, 'Just wait fora da tunnel, Giuseppe. They'll soon enough shutta da windows then!'

Antonio had no love for his country's allies. His younger sister had been savagely beaten·up·by a drunken Wehrmacht corporal only last year and, if it had not been for his wretched flat feet, he would have long ago joined his partisan friends who had taken to the hills shortly after Italy declared war. He was still thinking about this when he turned to look forward through one of the circular portholes in front of the driver's cabin. The cutting was coming closer. It was Giuseppe's warning shout which snapped him out of his reverie.

'Looka over there, Antonio. Look! Spitfieri!'

The driver reached for the throttle lever and managed to coax a few more revs out of his ageing locomotive.

*

As the tall cliffs of Sicily rapidly approached, I gave the signal to Tommy that now was the time to break cover and climb to one thousand feet. The ground fell away quickly as my eyes swept the surrounding area, hoping to spot a likely target. We were flying one of the 'Rhubarb' sorties when two fighters took off to range freely over a given area to attack any worthwhile military targets they came upon. However the success of these missions depended largely on being able to surprise the enemy before he could warn his defences to be on the alert. It is doubtful whether the 'Rhubarb' sorties were of any great military importance, although they must have been thorns in the sides of Germans and Italians alike. However, they were certainly doing much to boost the morale of our own chaps – particularly after the severe restrictions of the past six months.

Until December, no ships had been able to reach Malta since the ill-fated August convoy and consequently the island went short of everything – food, fuel, ammunition – all had to be strictly rationed. Even the five Spitfire squadrons on which the air defence' of the island depended, had had to be restricted to one sortie per aircraft per day, when pilots were required to switch off their engines immediately after touch-down and be pushed to protective dispersals by whoever happened to be on hand at the time. The reverse procedure was adopted before taking off – the aircraft being manhandled to the nearest end of the runway by ground crews, after which it became a toss-up whether they got airborne into wind or downwind.

The ack-ack defences too were affected, and General Beckett's boys were only allowed to fire off their daily ration of shells, no matter how heavy was the raid. As for transportation, only those vehicles considered absolutely necessary for the continuing survival of the island got any petrol, otherwise it became a matter of using one's two feet or, at best, a bicycle. Any animals on four legs had long since been eaten.

However, things were better and we could now afford to take an occasional stab at the enemy on his home ground. Hence the somewhat amateurish, but most invigorating, attempts to swing over to the offensive.

Tommy spotted the train first.

'Hello One Five. Train at three o'clock. Do you see it?'

'Roger Two Seven. Let's have a go!'

The train was disappearing into a deep cutting by the time we had swung round, but puffs of white smoke continued to give away its position. I turned the safety ring to the 'fire' position as we climbed to make our attack, but we failed to get there before the last coach disappeared into a tunnel.

'Hello Two Seven. We'll wait for it to come out at the other end!'

We could see the end of the tunnel about a half mile to the West and throttled back in a wide circuit to get into position for an attack whenever the train emerged. We continued to circle. Then round again, but still our quarry failed to appear. It seemed Giuseppe had sensibly chosen to hole-up where it was safe!

As it was likely our presence over Sicily had been reported, we moved off in a north-easterly direction, weaving this way and that to make it more difficult for any lurking gun sites to take their toll, all the while scanning the ground ahead for likely targets, but without spotting any. Just when I had decided we had gone far enough inland and ought to be turning back, we spotted a cloud of dust rising from behind a distant hedgerow. We turned in its direction.

'It's a staff car, Two Seven. You go left. I'll come in from the right!'

I watched Tommy's Spitfire climbing away, its twin cannons outlined against the clouds, and took up position well to the right of the speeding car. We turned inwards at the same time, one from each side of the road, and pressed our firing buttons.

Choomph – choomph – choomph ...

The Spitfire shuddered under the recoil from the cannon fire as the shells burst across a field and on to the road ahead of the dark green car, three of its four occupants staring up in our direction. Further puffs of debris coming from the other side confirmed that Tommy was also on target. Suddenly our quarry swerved violently and crashed into a ditch, when the last I saw, on sweeping low across it, were the rear doors of the car swinging open and two figures leaping from the vehicle and scampering off into a clump of nearby bushes. Now it was definitely time to head for home and I called my colleague to tuck himself in beside me.

It was disappointing the sortie had not borne more fruit. Also the incident with the train was still rankling! Nevertheless it would have been unwise to have gone looking for it, for I had caught sight of the flak truck before it disappeared into the tunnel and its crew would undoubtedly be waiting for us if we turned up again. So we made for the coast and crossed it some twenty miles from where we had come in. A few small fishing caiques drifted aimlessly offshore but a larger vessel was steaming in an easterly direction about a mile further out. We would take a look, just in case. Our luck was in.

The ship turned out to be a small armed coaster, probably commandeered for the duration to ferry war supplies round the coast. It appeared to be heading towards Catania, where the Luftwaffe had a large air base – at least that was what we had decided as we lined up to attack. Feverish activity broke out on deck as the crew rushed to their action stations and I saw two leap overboard as soon as our shells began to strike just aft of the wheelhouse. Simultaneously, puffs of smoke burst around us as the ship's gunners started to fire back, but they must have had an attack of the jitters, for we got away unscathed.

We returned to base without further incident, although we saw a number of Me 109's circling high above as we sped southwards at full throttle only a few feet above the waves. The Spitfire's dark green camouflage must have made us difficult to spot against the sea.

*

We were about to pack up for lunch when the AOC's little red MG drew up outside the crew room. Frank had not warned me to expect a visit from Keith Park so I told Tommy to ring and warn him that Father was here, whilst I went out to greet him. Frank and I had moved to Krendi two weeks before, he as the Station Commander and I as Wing Leader.

'Good afternoon, gentlemen. I thought it about time I visited you in your new quarters. How are you getting along? Ah, there you are, Tyson. I'm sorry not to have let you know I was coming, but I was calling on the Governor and thought I would look in here on my way back. In any case, there is a job I want your boys to do. I hope they have been getting in plenty of bombing practice!'

The AOC outlined a plan for carrying out a worthwhile raid on enemy territory which would call for the employment of an entire squadron of Spitfire Bombers and went on to say that his staff had been evaluating a number of possible targets. He was detailing the Krendi Wing for the job as most of our aircraft had been modified to carry bombs, and ended by saying that we could expect a visit from the Intelligence Officer within the next few days.

The IO arrived carrying a large cardboard folder. We stood around as he spread a large-scale map of southern Sicily on the table and placed a number of aerial photographs beside it. These showed a large barn-like building which, he assured us, was actually a factory engaged in the manufacture of chemicals – chiefly nitrates. It was situated in open country about five miles from the town of Pochino, and the more we studied it, the more we liked it. In fact, it looked an ideal target on which to try out our new weapons in anger, for it would be easy to spot from the air and, as far as we could see, the photographs revealed no concentrations of flak nearby. We thanked our Intelligence friend and sat down to work out our tactics.

The outcome made sense. Tommy Smart would lead the twelve bombed-up Spitfires with 229 Squadron but, as they would be vulnerable to attack by enemy fighters on the way over, I would provide him with a close escort of twelve un-bombed aircraft from 249 Squadron and maintain a top cover whilst they went down to deliver their loads. Once this was completed, 249 Squadron would come down and strafe the target with cannon and machine gun fire and thereafter be escorted back to base by Tommy's outfit, which would still have its ammunition intact.

*

As the target was situated near the coast, we had to climb to height considerably earlier than we were used to, with the result that the defending fighters would have received plenty of warning of our approach. Thus we were very much on the qui vive by the time we reached our bombing height of 10,000 feet surprised, but relieved, to find the sky still free of enemy aircraft. We flew in a wide arc and watched Tommy's squadron roll over in quick succession and plummet straight towards the ground.

As soon as the last 229 aircraft disappeared, I called 249 into line astern and dived after it, swinging in a wide spiral to approach the target from the north and at ground level. Everything happened at breakneck speed from then on as we streaked across the countryside at low level towards the building, black smoke already billowing through its open door. It became a fleeting kaleidoscope of impressions – a small knot of people standing by a roadside and pointing at us; an electricity pylon flashing by uncomfortably close to my starboard wingtip; a tall wooden flak tower to the right – where had it come from? – the gaping door of the factory itself, behind which I could see short red flashes caused by cannon shells exploding on the wall at the rear; a sudden eruption of steam as a boiler blew up; a donkey harnessed to a small cart rearing in the air, either in fright or because the unfortunate animal had stopped a stray bullet. It was all over in a jiffy and I continued to roar over the fields at full speed with the others following close behind. The Spitfire juddered when the engine started to run rough. Then it gave an alarming cough.

It was as if a giant's hand had reached down from the sky and was trying to pull the aircraft to a full stop. Puffs of dark smoke streamed from the exhaust stubs as the engine continued to misfire, and I suspected that my coolant tank had been pierced and that the engine was overheating. However a quick glance at the instruments assured me that the temperatures and pressures were registering correctly, although the aircraft was losing so much power that I would surely have to come down – and soon. But I was flying too low to bale out safely and it would have to be a forced landing, wheels up, with the sure prospect of falling into enemy hands.

While searching for a suitable field in which to come down, I called the boys on the radio to carry on without me and not to hang about. After all, they could not help, as they had already used up their ammunition on the factory and it would only be a matter of time before enemy fighters turned up at the scene. So off they went.

They had no sooner departed when a red light flashing on the instrument panel caught my eye. Insufficient fuel – that was it! Fuel starvation. There must be a blockage somewhere.

I had to release my safety harness to stretch far enough forward to reach the priming plunger but, as soon as I unscrewed it and began pumping more petrol into the engine, it picked up and went on running so long as the propeller was kept in fine pitch and I did not stop forcing in more fuel.

Thus I continued over the coast, vulnerable and exposed, while the faithful Spitfire coughed and spluttered its way across that interminable stretch of water, pouring out yards of black smoke for all the world to see. As expected, the Messerschmitt circus was in position up top, but again it failed to spot me against the dark coloured background. I finally reached Krendi half an hour after the last of my colleagues had landed.

'Oh, it's you, is it? We thought you were going down. Hey, Tommy – you are *not* taking over the Wing after all!'

Some welcome! There were some who reckoned this type of sortie boded well for promotion!

19

A SINGLE TO BLIGHTY

The faint smell of ether was everywhere; it even permeated the side ward in spite of the large window being kept open. Prosser Hanks threw his cap on the end of the bed.

'God, you never seem to get away from it! It's the same in every hospital I visit, and it always makes me feel queezy. But how are you, you old fraud? They tell me you've been quite ill. What was it? The dreaded pox?'

'I don't think they are quite sure yet, Prosser. The docs keep coming in to take samples of blood, but all they've told me so far is that my teeter is rising!'

The loud guffaw and inevitable unprintable rejoinder was interrupted by the arrival of Sister McLean carrying a tea tray.

'Here's a pot of tea for your visitor, Wing Commander. It's a good old Army brew made specially for the occasion.'

Prosser looked up.

'Tea? I never touch the stuff, Sister, but thank you very much just the same.'

Sister gave me a wink and, ignoring the criticism, proceeded to pour out a cupful of the amber-coloured liquid.

'You ought to try some, but you'll find it better without milk or sugar.'

Prosser shot a baleful look but, at a nod from me, lifted the cup to his lips. Poor old Sandy, you could almost see him thinking, having to humour the old dear like this. But his expression altered when he smelt the contents. Indeed, he rose at once to plant a smacking kiss on Sister's forehead.

'Sister, I take back all I said – You are an angel! Thank you very much indeed.'

This was only one of Sister McLean's special surprises, for she was for ever popping into the ward with little titbits; an odd chocolate biscuit or a macaroon; a newly published novel; the occasional glass of spirits. She knew what made the chaps tick and was well aware that my visitor would hardly relish anything so insipid as a cup of tea after making the journey all the way from Halfar just to visit his old chum Johnstone. I never found out whence she came by the stocks, but she always managed to produce the pot of whisky whenever anyone called to see me and it had not taken long to realise that the constant stream of well-wishers had little to do with personal popularity!

*

The deprivations of the past nine months had taken their toll in Malta by the beginning of 1943, for the chronic shortage of wholesome food had undermined the constitutions of all but the healthiest, and a variety of diseases had erupted throughout the island. The majority of the females in the Operations Room, for instance, suffered some form of skin complaint or other, probably picked up from contaminated headsets as their watches changed over. Outbreaks of eczema and impetigo became endemic among the girls in spite of every attempt being made to clean their telephones as often as possible, even sacrificing our last bottle of whisky for use as a disinfectant on one occasion, the stocks of lysol having long since run out. Lately, too, a serious outbreak of poliomyelitis had forced the Governor to close all places of entertainment, and further steps were taken to make it illegal for groups of more than four to congregate anywhere. Of course, the troops became very vulnerable in their crowded sleeping quarters and, in spite of the cold conditions of the winter months, windows and doors had to remain open also, in spite of the havoc it played with blackout arrangements. It was not surprising, therefore, that many of the lads caught the disease.

I had been feeling off-colour for several days before waking one night with a splitting headache and a feeling of stiffness in the limbs and down my back, and did not wait for dawn to break before hastily dressing and driving myself to the military hospital. Naturally I suspected the worst. However the duty medical officer was kindness itself as he carried out a thorough examination. He rose from the couch and removed his stethoscope.

'I'm pretty sure it's not polio, Sir, but I cannot tell at this stage what it is you've got. However you must stay here for the time being, for you are running a high temperature and it would be unwise to go back to Krendi. I'll arrange for someone to pick up your car and, in the meantime, Sister will take you to your room and I will look in and see you later.'

Thus I found myself the occupant of a pleasant room in the Army hospital at Imtarfa overlooking the recently abandoned airfield at Takali; abandoned because its continuing use as an operational base was attracting too much attention from enemy bombers and putting the hospital at additional risk. The Spitfire squadrons had moved from there to Krendi at the time I took over the Wing.

The doctors seemed unduly persistent.

'Have you been drinking milk, Johnstone?'

I assured them I had not. It was not my tipple and, in any case, it was being continually drummed into us that we should never drink milk in Malta, for the island goats had a notorious reputation for brucillosis.

'But think back, man – when did you last drink any? You must have done – and recently too!'

Bit by bit my gastronomic habits were unravelled as I racked my brain to remember what sort of diet I had followed since arriving in the Middle East. One thing was certain – I had not had an opportunity to quaff any of the white stuff since arriving in Malta, even if I had wanted to, nor did I remember having done so during my stay in Palestine. However, I mentioned a propensity of mine for eating fresh cheese turned out from a little rubber bag slung round a goat's udders which used to call regularly at my flat in Beirut, at which revelation I was put through a searching examination of my health record since that time. Certainly there had been periods when I had not been feeling up to the mark, but at the time I had merely put them down to a surfeit of good living. That was it, they told me. I had undulant fever and the best, and indeed the only, cure was to get away from the Mediterranean area as soon as possible. Thus I was medically boarded and ordered to return to the U.K.

*

The RAF fellows were not slow to take up the vacancies in the Union Club's membership created when the Royal Navy had been forced to withdraw temporarily from Malta, and this fine establishment had become the focal point of our leisure moments ever since. It was not unnatural, therefore, that this, on my last night on the island, should be the venue for my farewell party. What my well-wishers overlooked, however, was that it was also my first night out of hospital after four weeks in bed and that my constitution was sadly out of training for the generous hospitality to which I was treated. My recollection of the events which followed are understandably hazy.

My flight was due to take off at midnight, a detail of which, I am pleased to say, my mentors had taken due note. Around ten thirty, therefore, it was agreed that it was time to drive me to the airfield. However, as we lurched from the Club into a starless night, the party became separated in the blackout and Pete Wykeham-Barnes had difficulty locating me. When he did, however, Pete said I was showing considerable reluctance to leave the island and had to be forcibly bundled into his car and sat on during the ride to the aerodrome. Having dumped me unceremoniously outside the entrance to G Shelter and having called a cursory farewell, he and his companion drove off in the direction of the officers' mess.

'Heavens, you would think he didn't want to go home, the stupid clot! Fighting like a wild animal he was! However, he should be all right now. Let's nip over to the Mess and see whether they can rustle up a few sandwiches for us. I could do with something to eat before turning in.'

They strolled into the anteroom and called for the mess

steward. Prosser suddenly caught Pete's arm and pointed to the two figures sitting at a table in the corner of the room, a plateful of sandwiches in front of them.

'I just don't believe it! How the hell has he got here?'

Mike Stephens called to them to join us.

'Where have you been? I found Sandy weaving up the Strada Realle and brought him back with me. I thought he ought to have something to eat before he sets off. I was just about to come looking for you in case your car had broken down!'

Prosser and Pete looked at each other.

'Oh, my God! I wonder who we kidnapped! No wonder the poor sod didn't want to come with us!'

They never did find out whom they had abducted from the streets of Valletta and abandoned in the middle of the airfield that night. Some unfortunate civilian, no doubt, who thus found himself marooned at Luqa with the prospect of a four mile walk home. However, I was there and, thanks to Mike's thoughtfulness in providing the sandwiches, was able to make my departure in a comparatively orthodox fashion in due course.

Sleep overtook me almost as soon as the lights of the flarepath had disappeared and I did not wake again until the high snow-covered peaks of the Sierra Nevada were appearing through the early morning haze. A throbbing head and a dry mouth bore ample testimony to the well-meant ministrations of the night before, but otherwise I seemed to be all in one piece. A painful look round the cabin revealed three other occupants, all of whom had at least one limb encased in plaster, having become victims of the dreaded poliomyelitis. Unfortunately I chose to stand up at the same time as one of my travelling companions whose arm had been plastered in an outright position, when he clouted me over the head with it as he turned to say hello, whereupon I subsided into my seat, to remain there until we were safely on the ground at Gibraltar.

It was four days before an onward passage could be arranged for us, during which I was free to enjoy what the garrison had to offer. The absence of blackout and a plentiful supply of food worked wonders. Although the rock was so full of troops in transit to North Africa that it was impossible to obtain entry to any place of entertainment without booking at least one week in advance. Furthermore, as the ratio of males to females was in the region of two hundred to one, it appeared that a similar system of partner reservation was in force, and therefore the time had to be spent in a fashion of which even my grandmother would have approved. Nevertheless it was an interesting spot.

The wide bay was full of Allied ships, so many that several seemed to be tied up at Algeciras itself. Dominating the scene was HMS *Nelson*, which had substituted herself for her sister-ship *Rodney* when the latter set sail in the dead of night to lend her might to the invasion forces at North Africa, thus deluding enemy spies into believing that no capital ships were involved. The recently constructed runway extending into the bay was in constant use as supply aircraft plied back and forth between Gibraltar and the other continent. But it was limited in length; too short, on occasions, for the safe operation of heavily laden transports. Indeed, a Liberator evacuating civilians from Malta had, only a few months previously, overshot the landing area and had run into the sea, when its entire civilian payload had been drowned.

My erstwhile travelling companions had had to remain in hospital during the sojourn in Gibraltar, but we were reunited when space was found for us in a Lockheed Hudson destined for the United Kingdom. Unfortunately, its crew were two Czechoslovaks, neither of whom could speak English, so we could do no more than come to a nodding acquaintance with them before the aircraft finally staggered off the end of the runway under a full load of petrol, just managing to clear the tall masts of many ships moored in the flight path. Heavy rain was falling at the time and it was not long before the lights of the Rock disappeared from sight, so we settled down for the night, praying inwardly that the Luftwaffe fighter pilots would be taking a day off by the time we had reached the Bay of Biscay, for several British aircraft had been shot down whilst traversing that vulnerable stretch of the flight.

Sleep was hard to come by as we droned northwards, especially as our crew seemed to be remarkably hamfisted on the controls, for the aircraft frequently gave a violent jerk when the pilot made a correction of course or hauled it up or down to correct the height level. The lights of Lisbon had twinkled their neutrality far off to the right before the arms of Morpheus took me into their comforting embrace.

When I awoke, dawn was breaking and we were flying in and out of broken clouds with nothing else but sea in sight. By my reckoning we should have been more than half way across the Bay – slap in the middle of the danger area. A visit to the flight deck was called for, but the sight that met me in the cockpit was hardly encouraging.

Both the pilot and navigator were fast asleep, their heads lolling on their chests, whilst the automatic pilot guided the aircraft along its jerky course. I shook the captain into some semblance of wakefulness and shouted to ask where we were, when he in turn shook his colleague, who merely yawned hugely and shrugged his shoulders.

'We go to England!' was all I could get out of him.

I returned to the cabin and resumed my prayers – it seemed the most productive thing to do in the circumstances – and forbore to say anything to the others; they already had enough with which to contend as it was. However, it was a comfort to know that our crew was at least awake now!

The weather grew steadily worse. Once we flew over a German E Boat whose crew thankfully ignored us as their craft sped towards the French coast, but that was the only shipping we spotted, although there could have been more hidden in the mists which now surrounded us. The flight seemed interminable.

Suddenly we were over land. Fields – beautiful green fields. Until that moment I had not appreciated how much greener the fields in England are than anywhere else in the world. It gave one a longing to get down and kiss the ground, a gesture hardly practicable in the circumstances.

Sounds of jubilation reached us from the cockpit and, on going forward, I found the pair of them shouting and gesticulating at each other as they endeavoured to plot our position on the map. Whilst this was going on we crossed the coast again, but not before I had fleetingly recognised the town of Newquay a mile to starboard. Only then did I discover we should be landing at Portreath when I was able, with much difficulty, to persuade the pilot to point the aircraft in a south-westerly direction and join the correct circuit. My joy at getting home was further enhanced on finding that Jack Boret was the Station Commander at Portreath, for I had not seen him since those far-off days at Tangmere.

After breakfasting in the mess with Jack and being processed through the personnel handling section, I was detailed to proceed to the Central Medical Establishment in London for boarding and further instructions. Discovering the Hudson was due to fly on to Hendon, I elected to travel in it in preference to an arduous journey by train, but I should have known better.

Hendon was surrounded by buildings and a railway embankment and was not an easy airfield to get into at any time and it would certainly require careful handling to get a Hudson safely down. I sincerely hoped our friends from Czechoslovakia would be up to it. When coming in to land, therefore, my heart missed several beats when it was obvious they had forgotten to lower the landing flaps as the ground rushed up to meet us.

We belted across the threshold like a cat out of hell and were nearly half way across the field before the wheels first made contact with the ground, after which the brakes were slammed on so viciously that the poor old aircraft nearly stood on its nose. Nearer and nearer came the far boundary whilst the aeroplane continued to bucket alarmingly towards the hedge. However the pilot was now committed to a landing and took the only course left to him – he swung the aircraft off the runway and into a wild ground loop, sending large dollops of soft mud cascading over the fuselage. It said much for the sturdiness of the landing gear that it did not fold up then and there, but we somehow got away with it and taxied to the hardstanding.

The navigator's beaming face appeared at the cockpit door.

'We go to England!'

After that, I only wanted to go to the Medical Establishment!

20

WHAT GOES UP

The masked headlights of the old ambulance barely gave off enough light to pick out the road leading to the station sick quarters, but the driver knew the way like the back of his hand and turned in at the right spot. He left the engine running when he ran to the back of the vehicle to help his mate off-load the stretcher cases whilst the walking injured made their own way inside, for he would have to return to the scene in case there were other casualties to bring back. He turned to his companion sitting alongside as they drove down the hill.

'It sounds as if they are having quite a party in the Nob's quarters tonight, Bill – you can hear the din from SHQ. Cor blimey, some have all the luck!'

The aged vehicle continued past the spur leading to the officers' mess, whence the sound of music and merriment could be clearly heard, whilst inside the building itself a party was in full swing, for the officers had invited some guests to an informal dance that evening and most had turned up. Fairwood Common was a popular venue with the local residents and few ever declined an invitation.

'Two whiskies and soda please, Jones. How much is that? Two bob – OK, hang on a moment.'

Bud Abbot tore two small perforated stamps from his book of wine chits and handed them to the barman before carrying the glasses across the room.

'Here's your drink, Mrs Agnew – Oh, I'm sorry, Sir, I didn't realise you had come back. What will you have?'

Her husband declined the offer.

'No thanks, old boy. But do you know where the Wing Commander is? He has been gone a long time and we ought to be leaving soon.'

'I gather there has been a spot of trouble on the airfield, Sir, but I don't think he will be long.'

The Station Commander walked into the gaily decorated anteroom soon after and made towards his guests.

'I'm sorry to have been away so long, but there has been a rather nasty accident up top, and I'm afraid I will have to leave you again. Sorry to be such a rotten host!'

'But you have blood on your face, Sandy. Are you all right? What's happened?'

'Yes, I'm perfectly all right, thank you Joy – it's probably off someone else. At the moment I'm not quite sure what caused it, but several girls have been hurt in an accident at the WAAF site and I must go back there straightaway. I'll telephone you in the morning if you have gone before I get back.'

*

Small groups of girls, wrapped in blankets, huddled together in the darkness whilst rescuers groped among the wreckage of their dormitories in search of anyone still trapped among the tangle of broken beams and bits of bedroom furniture. One building was on fire where a coal stove had been overturned and had set light to the wooden rafters lying across it. Pale shafts from the searchers' torches swung to and fro as heaps of rubble were cast aside when more helpers joined in, but this was the only illumination. My first impression, on reaching the eerie scene, was that the buildings had been struck by a bomb.

Stan Davies appeared like a wraith out of the smoke and dust.

'What the hell has happened, Dave? I didn't hear any air raid alert.'

Davies pointed to the adjacent field.

'Apparently a Halifax on two engines tried to land and stalled into the site. It's lying over there, but the crew seem to

ckleton Mk 1

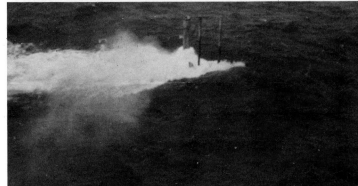

Submarine *Andrew*
ing the first undersea
ssing of the Atlantic in
3

views of the
ckleton Mk2 involved
é Autolycus exercise

Meteor Night Fighters Mk 11

Bill Kent, Jerry Roberts and I in Malta after our jet flight

be unhurt: In fact they had no idea they had hit anything! I've sent them over to sick quarters. Do you mind if I borrow your car to take these girls over, Sir? I'll bring some of the lads back with me, for we could do with more help here.'

It was daylight before we were satisfied that all the girls had been accounted for and were being properly looked after in the station hospital. It was a miracle that only two had suffered more than minor injuries, for a visit to the site next morning revealed their dormitory buildings reduced to rubble where the heavy four-engined bomber had scythed through them before crashing into the neighbouring field. Everything above bed-level had gone and it was fortunate the occupants had been lying down at the time, otherwise most would have had their heads knocked off. Two of the more seriously injured had been sent to the General Hospital in Swansea where one girl, alas, succumbed later that night.

*

It could be said that Fairwood Common was a classic example of shutting the stable door after the horse had bolted, for it was built after a devastating bombing raid on Swansea had generated so much rubble that, once carried away in lorries and tipped into a marsh on the Common, it had formed a sufficiently stable foundation in the morass on which to lay a runway. Only then was a fighter squadron based there for the air defence of the local area, after which, of course, the Luftwaffe had given the place a complete miss! The squadron currently at Fairwood was mostly engaged in training and in chasing desultory raids in the Bristol and Exeter areas.

Having recovered from the debilitating effects of undulant fever after returning from Malta, and being grounded long enough to complete a course at the Royal Air Force Staff College, I had been appointed to the post of Sector Commander in South Wales in October 1943. As the job also involved running the fighter wing, a Spitfire was established for my use and I was thus able to keep my hand in on the type whilst, at the same time, learning something of the intricacies of a Beaufighter in its night-fighting role. In the air, not much was happening locally during the early months of 1944, although there was plenty of activity on the ground while the Allied forces congregated in the area preparatory to being brought up to scratch for an invasion of the Continent, which everyone anticipated would happen soon.

Thus we had settled down to a fairly routine, but well-ordered, existence, apart from a regular incursion of sheep and wild ponies who found it more comfortable to bed down on our runways than in the damp fastness of their stretch of nearby moorland. The erection of a single-strand electrified wire round the perimeter failed to deter the animals; in fact, it had the opposite effect, for they turned up in ever increasing numbers to enjoy the tingling sensation they got when they rubbed their noses up and down the live wire.

And so 29th March began for me as many other days had done in the past, with an early briefing in the Operations Room, followed by a session in the office to clear outstanding paperwork. I had arranged to lunch with a friend at Pembrey and, although the weather was overcast with rain threatening at any moment, had decided to take the Spitfire and carry out some practice flying on the way over.

Meanwhile, Megan and Bridget were loading their mobile canteen in Sketty before setting out on their daily round of calls at the nearby service units. They enjoyed the job, for they were generally well received by the lads and it was nice to know they appreciated the service they provided.

'That's right, Bridget girl – put in an extra tray of doughnuts now, for you know how much they like them, see!'

Bridget handed up the long tray, loaded with freshly baked goodies, and looked round the interior to make sure nothing had been forgotten.

'I think that will do for today, won't it? We'll go by Gorseinon and see what the new Yankee boys are like. They tell me they are proper devils, they are! I hope they won't eat all the doughnuts though for, you see, I promised to take some to the boys at the aerodrome.'

Rain began falling as the unwieldy brown-coloured vehicle wended its way along the narrow roads leading to the Americans' camp, and Megan was hoping the extra journey would be worthwhile, for they had started earlier than usual today to make the additional call. A number of GI's gazed curiously at the van as it drew up alongside a group who were in the midst of putting up a collapsible wooden building. Two or three left the site and wandered over to accept the mugs which Bridget handed across the small counter. One of the crew-cut soldiers took a sip of the brew and promptly spat it on the ground.

'Gee, sister, aint ya gotten any cawfee? Ah jest caint be doin' with yer goddam English tea!'

There was a mumble of agreement from the others who thereupon replaced their full mugs on the shelf and went back to work without even bothering to find out what other wares were for sale in the van.

Megan's nose was high in the air as she started up and reversed out of the site, for she was much offended by the frosty reception and, besides, had taken exception to the reference to 'English tea'. She was a true-born Welshwoman, she was, and tea brewed in Wales was Welsh tea as far as she was concerned!

'It's bloody cheek, it is! Am I not glad now that we didn't let them see the doughnuts. At least we know where we are not wanted after that!'

The encounter was still rankling when they reached the sharp turn at Three Crosses and turned towards the airfield. It was now raining hard and the wipers were leaving oily smudges on the windscreen as the blades flipped back and forth, and Megan had to lean forward to keep the narrow road in sight when they came to the open stretch across the Common. Suddenly a figure at the end of a parachute thumped on to the ground alongside the slowly moving vehicle. Then another. And another.

Thinking an invasion had started, Megan stopped the van and stared in amazement as four men in flying kit picked themselves up from the ground and started to walk towards them, but she was nothing if not resourceful and had run to the back and opened the shutter before any of them had reached the canteen.

'This is, indeed to goodness, a pleasant surprise! You would care for some tea, of course!'

Four hands reached out and their owners gratefully sipped the steaming brew.

*

'Humbug Master. Humbug Master. We have a distress call from a Liberator which has got lost and is running short of fuel. I'm trying to bring him in, but am having difficulty getting a fix. Will you change over to World Guard and I'll try to vector you on to him. Over.'

Having changed radio frequencies and made new contact with the Fairwood tower, I could now listen to the anxious voice of the Liberator pilot crackling through a lot of background interference. He was on the point of acknowledging an instruction from the controller.

'Roger Control. We are in the soup now. Reducing to get below cloud.'

'You should be OK on present vector: Do not come below eight hundred feet: There is a hill between you and me.'

'The port inner has just stopped. We will stay up in case we have to bale out.'

'O.K. Steer zero three zero and give me a long transmission for fix.'

'Say again – I do not understand your message.'

'I say again – give me a long transmission and I will try to fix your position.'

It appeared the crippled bomber was still to the south of the airfield and I flew in that direction, nipping in and out of rain-filled clouds whose base was never more than six hundred feet. The controller now had me in radio contact but was still having trouble making the American understand his instructions. I decided to call the bomber myself.

'Hello Yankee Yoke. Hello Yankee Yoke. This is Humbug Master. I am in a Spitfire and will try to make contact with you to lead you down. Please give a long transmission so that Control can fix your position.'

'Roger Spitfire. Wilco. I've just seen some little lakes underneath. Does that help you? Aw hell, the port outer's quit on us now. We are running out of juice. Please hurry!'

The controller's voice broke into the conversation.

'O.K. Yankee Yoke. Start circling and let down below cloud. We can hear you overhead. We are firing lights. Keep turning to port.'

'We are turning to port. Yeah, we see the lights and turning on to runway. Am putting down the landing gear.'

Streaking across Caeffyn Bryn I was just in time to catch sight of the massive bulk of the American bomber breaking through the clouds, but clearly not lining up with either runway. In fact, the aircraft was over the airfield and turning towards the east.

'Hell, I've lost you again, Control. Where are your lights?'

'Keep turning. You have just passed overhead. Turn hard to port and come in on runway zero five. We are still firing flares.'

I opened up and made towards the field but, before reaching it, the bomber had climbed back into the clouds and disappeared from sight.

'Mayday! Mayday! Engines cutting. Am making height and baling out!'

Those watching in the tower stood transfixed as the large aircraft reappeared not more than three hundred feet above their heads, when four figures hurtled from the fuselage and dropped from their view behind the hangars without any sign of their parachutes having opened. The Liberator continued to bank steeply and appeared to be trying to line itself up with the shorter of the two runways. But it was in a hopeless position for landing and after bouncing heavily near the end of the runway, it careered through a fence and on into a deep ditch bordered by a heavy thicket hedge. It was not till then the controller realised there was someone still at the controls.

'My God! Get the ambulance over there quickly. Leave the others for the time being. They're probably beyond medical care anyway, for none of the parachutes opened.'

The ambulance had been summoned to the tower as soon as the emergency began and took no time to reach the crashed bomber, arriving just as the captain was helping an injured colleague to crawl through the battered nose of the aircraft.

Fortunately the empty fuel tanks cut down the risk of fire.

Meanwhile Stan Davies had driven off in the direction he had watched the bodies falling, although he was apprehensive about what he might find when he got there. He slowed down to turn on to the road across the Common and was surprised to see the YMCA wagon parked at the side of the road with four fellows alongside it, each clutching a mug in his hand and apparently chatting up the girls inside. As he climbed out of the car, he noticed a number of sodden parachute canopies lying out on the heath. The tallest of the four turned as he approached, a wide grin spreading across his features.

'Gee Bud, this is mighty fine tea you guys have over here!'

Megan and Bridget were smiling as well.

*

Lieutenant Helmberger was clearly a shaken man, but the third large scotch was beginning to take effect.

'Say Commander, I want to thank your guys for trying to help us down. It wasn't their fault we missed the runway, but I couldn't turn quickly enough – the gas drained from the engines every time I put a wing over. We were clean out of fuel, ah guess. And, gee, weren't these other guys lucky that their chutes opened just before they hit the deck!'

Our American colleagues had had a narrow escape and everyone was relieved the outcome had not been more serious, although the injured crew member eventually died from his injuries the following day. In the meantime, however, they were enjoying our hospitality, which we were equally pleased to dispense. Indeed, we were always happy to entertain visitors to Fairwood Common although, in the cases of the last two planeloads, we may have appreciated their company even more if they had only taken the trouble to arrive in a more orthodox manner!

21

THE VIP's

The Aide-de-Camp's head appeared round the half open
door.

'The Chief wants to see you, Sir!'

'Who did you say?'

'The Chief – L.M. Can you come down now, Sir? He's due
at Uxbridge in half an hour.'

Tony Dotteridge looked up from his files, a mischievous
grin spreading across his rugged features.

'What have you been up to this time, Sandy? It must be
something serious if the Old Man wants to see you personally.
I'll keep my fingers crossed for you!'

I was curious, and not a little disturbed, at being
summoned to the Holy of Holies for, although I had met Air
Chief Marshal Sir Trafford Leigh-Mallory briefly during his
visits to The War Room, our exchanges on these occasions
had been confined to everyday pleasantries, and anything to
do with the prosecution of the war had hitherto been the
province of my immediate boss, the Senior Air Staff Officer. It
was therefore a rather nervous young Group Captain who
straightened his tie before entering the outer office to be
invited to take a chair by one of the lady secretaries.

'I'm not sure what he wants to see you about,' she said, 'He
was saying something about paying a visit to the other side
and he probably wants you to arrange an aircraft to take him
over. Hang on a moment and I'll see if he's free now ...'

The Commander-in-Chief looked up as I entered.

'Ah, it's you, Johnstone. Come in! They tell me a new

Mosquito has just been delivered to the Com Flight. I want you to fly me over to LG4 in it this afternoon. I must be there at two o'clock at the latest, so we'll meet at Heston for take-off at one sharp! I have a meeting at Uxbridge this morning, so I'll join you at the aircraft. You had better have lunch before you leave. I will bring sandwiches with me.'

It was on the tip of my tongue to confess, but something told me to hold my counsel and chance it. After all, it was an opportunity not to be missed! So, having assured him I would be there on time, I left the office in even greater trepidation than when entering it, and made for my own. Naturally it was thrilling to be asked to pilot the Chief, but I had considerable qualms about taking on the job. Unfortunately I had never flown a Mosquito!

'Tony, let me have the Handling Notes on the Mossie, for I'll need to mug them up. L.M. wants me to take him over to France in one this afternoon!'

Dotteridge's face was a picture.

'He wants you to do *what?*' he exploded.

*

I had been appointed Group Captain Operations at the Headquarters of the Allied Expeditionary Air Force at Stanmore in May 1944 and, among the tasks which fell on my plate was to supervise the re-equipment programme of the fighter squadrons earmarked for the Invasion of Europe. Thus when a batch of new Mosquito sixes became available for distribution, I had been able to allocate one to our Communications Flight based at the now defunct grass airfield at Heston, where I left instructions that no one was to fly it until I could find time to try it out for myself. Now I had been well and truly hoist with my own petard!

Nothing ventured, however, and having armed myself with a copy of the Handling Notes, I repaired to the 'Puddle Jumper' strip and was flown in an Auster to Heston, where I made directly for the Mosquito. It did not take long to become familiar with the controls and switches and everything was going swimmingly until the starboard engine started up with an almighty backfire which was followed by a volume of thick black smoke. However, the attendant engineering staff soon had the cowlings off and put right whatever had been at fault, when I was able to complete the run-up sequences and switch off to await the arrival of L.M.

To get into the cockpit of a Mosquito it is necessary to climb a telescopic ladder and squeeze through a small hatchway cut out of the side of the fuselage and, once inside, there is just enough space for two medium-sized persons to sit side by side. However, L.M. was no sylph and found it more comfortable to take off his tunic and bulky life jacket before being strapped in beside me.

Thus we taxied slowly to the far end of the field when the ground controller flashed us permission to take off. L.M. was undoing his packet of sandwiches as I eased open the throttles and the Mosquito rapidly gathered speed for the take-off.

At this point I began to realise that the Handling Notes, although adequate for all purposes up to the moment of starting engines, were singularly devoid of hints on how to fly the aeroplane itself, for we began to develop a swing to the left which became more and more difficult to control, the faster we went. Indeed, the take-off was a veritable nightmare, which only ended when we just managed to squeeze between two hangars situated at right angles to our intended flight path. L.M. hastily laid aside his sandwiches.

'Of course, Johnstone, you used to command a Mosquito squadron, didn't you?'

The moment of truth had arrived.

'No, Sir – I've never flown one before!'

The man must have had nerves of steel, for he made no further comment and merely resumed his frugal lunch as we flew low over the sea towards the coast of Normandy. We could see above us a number of Allied fighters maintaining standing patrols over the myriad of ships plying back and forth across the Channel, bringing in more troops and materials or evacuating the casualties. Ahead the beaches loomed closer and, as we had time in hand, L.M. suggested we took a look at the British sector. So we altered course over the area where, ten days previously, our forces had stormed ashore under a murderous hail of fire from the defending Germans. Wrecks of ships and landing craft littered the beaches, whilst the burnt-out shells of many armoured vehicles bore witness of the bitter fighting which had taken place. To our right, however, we looked down on the heartening sight of a seemingly endless stream of trucks and armour rolling ashore along the sagging pontoons of the Mulberry harbour, an untidy string of scuppered merchantmen forming an effective breakwater at its outer limit. Fortunately no enemy fighters were about as we circled the awe-inspiring scene before turning on to an easterly course to locate the landing strip which teams from the RAF Airfield Construction Wing had recently hewn out of the countryside near the village of Balleroy.

These landing grounds, or LG's as they were known, had been constructed in haste and consisted only of a prepared surface on which pierced steel matting had been placed. As there had been little or no rain during the past week, they were now covered with a layer of fine dust, a matter of some concern to pilots using them as the dust clouds generated on take-off and landing were a complete give-away to any enemy aircraft which happened to be in the vicinity at the time. Six strips had been built so far, but none were yet manned by a permanent ground staff, and squadrons of the Tactical Air Force which had used them from time to time had always brought with them their own ground servicing personnel.

LG4 was unoccupied when we touched down and taxied to the far end of the dusty strip. Indeed, no one appeared to be there at all. This was surprising, for Air Vice Marshal Strafford and other senior officers had been instructed to meet L.M. there, as the purpose of the visit was for him to take part in a high-level conference to do with the immediate conduct of operations. Then a figure emerged from behind a tree. He was an American GI who slouched slowly towards us as I stopped both engines and clipped on the ladder to allow L.M. to climb down. He seemed to disappear over the side rather rapidly.

I even heard the thump from my elevated position in the cockpit and, on leaning through the exit door, was just in time to witness the C-in-C being hauled to his feet by our American friend, who was grinning broadly as he started to dust him down.

'Hard fall that, Buddy!' was his only comment.

Of course, as L.M. was still in his shirt sleeves, the GI was quite unaware of the identity of my passenger and, for all he knew, it could just as easily have been Bing Crosby or Tuesday Morning who had fallen at his feet! Therefore, in an attempt to redress the situation, I handed out the Chief's brass hat, but that, too, fell in the dust and it was only when I started to descend the ladder myself I realised it had not been fully extended, and had therefore swung violently beneath the fuselage as soon as L.M. had put his weight on it. It was some arrival!

Not unnaturally, the Chief was somewhat disgruntled as I was helping him into his tunic.

'Where the hell is Strafford? I told him to meet me here at two. What's the time now?'

'Five past,' I answered, looking at my watch. Then, turning to the American. 'This *is* LG4, I hope!'

'Could be, Bud – but there ain't no one here. Ah've gotten separated from ma outfit and jest happened to be passin' by!'

Further disorder was avoided when a dust cloud moving behind a hedge heralded the arrival of a staff car, out of which stepped Air Marshal Strafford and General de Guingand.

'We are sorry to be late, Sir. We went to the wrong LG but fortunately saw the Mossie turning over here and realised our mistake!'

At least that let me off the hook, for I was beginning to think it was me who had made the mistake and had come to the wrong LG. It would not have surprised me if I had, for I had long since realised it was going to be one of those days!

We drove off rapidly in the direction of Caen, but had some difficulty negotiating the wrecks of vehicles put out of action in the fighting. It was noticeable that many bore markings of German units, although of British manufacture, and one could only surmise they had fallen into enemy hands at the time of Dunkirk and had been used by them ever since. We eventually turned into a large field where a number of mobile office trailers denoted the temporary headquarters of the

Second Tactical Air Force.

A continuous rumble of heavy gunfire could be heard as we stepped from the car to be greeted by Air Marshal Sir Arthur Conningham and other senior officers. Apparently the town of Caen was proving a hard nut to crack and its stubborn defence by the enemy was causing a severe hold-up to the progress of Montgomery's Army. This then was the purpose of the meeting – to lay on a knock-out blow to clear the way for an advance eastward and towards Paris itself.

Someone produced a large-scale map of the district, with the positions of all engaged forces clearly marked on it, when Loel Guinness and I were bidden to hold it straight whilst the Generals and Air Marshals studied the dispositions. The meeting was taking place in the middle of an orchard, and Loel and I glanced apprehensively at the heavy black clouds which were gathering overhead and bringing with them a noticeable increase in the wind strength. Indeed we were already battling hard to keep the map sufficiently rigid for the party to make sense from it when an unexpected gust tore it from our grasp, leaving Loel and me each with a torn-off corner in our hands. The precious map took off, cleared the orchard and disappeared in the direction of the next field, hotly pursued by two Air Marshals, three Generals, two Group Captains and a Flight Lieutenant who only succeeded in capturing the document when it became entangled in the branches of a far-off cypress!

The rain was now coming down in buckets and I was worrying about the return flight, for a quick telephone call to Heston confirmed that conditions there were equally bad. Furthermore, I was not looking forward to the take-off before finding out what to do about the vicious swing. However, during a lull in the proceedings, I was able to pick the brains of Conningham's ADC, who had been a Mosquito pilot before joining his august master. Apparently the trick was to hold the tail down until almost airborne, so I repaired to LG4 with that worry at least removed from my mind. Nevertheless I was most unhappy about the weather, and told L.M. so. However, he was anxious to get back as he had pressing engagements later that evening, so we agreed to have a go, even if we had to land on an airfield on the South Coast.

Having this time negotiated the take-off successfully, we headed for the Channel, only to be met by a solid wall of black clouds which forced us to fly very low over the sea. As soon as we reached the English coast it was apparent that it would be foolhardy to fly inland, as there were no ground aids to help us. It was time to call it a day.

The fellows at RAF Ford rallied round magnificently and, after producing a cup of tea and biscuits, had the Chief despatched in the CO's car within twenty minutes from the time of our touchdown. I had taken the precaution beforehand to check with the driver that he knew the way to Bentley Priory, as it was all too easy to lose one's way in the dark, with no signposts to mark the route. I felt I could relax at last.

*

'I hope you got back all right last Friday, Sir!'

To my surprise, I was again in the Chief's office arranging the details of another trip in the Mosquito. L.M. glowered at me over the top of his spectacles.

'Don't dare talk to me about last Friday, Johnstone. I thought I knew a short cut ...! It was nearly midnight before we got back here! However, about tomorrow's trip ...'

I took down notes as he rattled off the details. Then L.M. looked up with a smile.

'– and this time make sure our departure signal says there will be a VVIP and a VIP on board!'

Wartime regulations forbade the names of passengers to be shown on movement signals – only their category of importance could be stated, if they merited the distinction. Three-star officers, senior Civil Servants, bishops and the like were designated VIP's. Only Royalty, The Prime Minister and a few very senior officers merited the double 'V'.

'I beg your pardon, Sir. Did I hear you say one VVIP and one VIP? I realise that you are a very, very important person, but I would hardly rate myself as even an important one!'

'Who said you were, Johnstone? In your case it stands for a Very Inexperienced Pilot!'

Indeed, that man *must* have had nerves of steel, for we VIP's flew together on numerous subsequent occasions.

22

WEB FEET

Commander Toby Weston leant over the navigation officer's shoulder whilst the latter completed his plot, then looked across to check the time on the ship's chronometer. It was coming up to nine-forty and, as the rendezvous was scheduled for ten o'clock, he would have to get a move on. He shifted to stand behind the coxswain as he studied the dials mounted on the bulkhead whilst, further aft, the Chief Engineer was making one of his regular rounds of the engines, checking pressure gauges and the revolution counters, and here and there laying a hand on the heavy steel casings to make sure no bearings were overheating. It was stuffy in the engineroom and the Chief looked at his watch while wiping his hands on a piece of cotton waste for he, too, knew they were due to surface soon and he was looking forward to a spell in the open air. But it had been a comparatively comfortable voyage so far and he was glad the skipper had taken the boat deep enough to get below the uncomfortable effects of the heavy swell they had been encountering while crossing the Bay.

Weston turned to his First Officer.

'O.K., Number One. Take her up!'

Warning bells sounded throughout the boat as the needles on the depth gauge and inclinometer started to register the change of attitude as tanks were blown and Her Majesty's submarine *Auriga* surged towards the surface.

'That's good, Number One! Up periscope.'

Commander Weston unclipped the handle-grips and moved slowly round the base of the periscope as he bent over to peer

into the eyepieces. He was satisfied there was no shipping in
the immediate vicinity.

'Rightio then, switch to diesels and open the hatches.'

As the large unlocking wheels were spun to release the
hatch locks a loud hissing sound heralded the welcome inrush
of fresh air. Toby slapped down the handle-grips and made for
the ladder leading to the conning tower, breathing deeply as
he stepped on to the bridge and felt the wind striking against
his cheeks. He glanced at his watch.

'They should be here in less than ten minutes. They've
always managed to make it on time so far. Look, I think I see
them – over there ...'

Pointing to the north, they saw a tiny speck in the sky
growing rapidly larger as it flew towards them. Soon the
unmistakable outline of a maritime aircraft confirmed it was
the Shackleton they had been expecting and they watched it
fly overhead and dip a wing to acknowledge their contact
before moving off to line up for another run over the
submarine. Toby grinned as he watched the large bomb doors
of the aircraft open wide to reveal a variety of stores mounted
on the racks. He looked again at his watch.

'Spot on!'

Things were not quite so easy up top, for I was having to
shield my eyes against the sun to keep the thin silhouette of
the conning tower in view. The strong light glinting on the sea
was making it difficult to keep in sight.

'Stand by in the nose, bomb aimer. Target coming up now.
It's all yours!'

Jock Gray pressed the release button and crawled back into
the cockpit, when he gave me a thumbs-up sign.

'Container away, Sir. It should be OK!'

The Shackleton swung round in a wide arc to port when I
was just in time to watch the metal cylinder, with its small
stabilising parachute streaming behind, strike the water about
a mile ahead of *Auriga*, whilst the sub slowed down to allow
two ratings armed with long boathooks to scamper along the
catwalk to hoist it on board when it came alongside.

'Well done, Jock! Another delivery tomorrow should be
sufficient. We'll take the rest down to Gib with us on

Thursday, for they should have arrived by then. In the meantime, let's go after the other fellow. What's my course?'

*

This was a far cry from the exhilaration and excitement one experienced in the cockpit of a single-seater fighter. Indeed it was a complete metamorphosis as far as I was concerned for, instead of having only myself to' worry about, I now found myself the captain of a multi-engined maritime aircraft carrying a crew of anything from eight to twelve, depending on the job we were doing. Nonetheless it was very interesting.

It was 1952 and the war had been over for seven years. The Powers That Be had been misguided enough to offer me a permanent commission in the Royal Air Force at the conclusion of hostilities, an offer I was quick to accept with gratitude, after which it had been thought advisable to broaden my experience for the years to follow. I had thus found myself the Air·Attaché in Dublin for two and a half years – an appointment which all but ruined me financially as well as physically – followed by a three year spell in the Air Ministry, before being put in charge of the unit responsible for evaluating the development work undertaken on behalf of Coastal Command. Consequently I had been taught the technique of flying large four-engined aircraft, such as Lancasters and Shackletons.

The Air/Sea Development Unit had many new types of undersea detection devices to try out and, as the work called for close liaison with our naval colleagues, one of Her Majesty's submarines would be detailed to collaborate with us whenever needed. We were therefore delighted when *Auriga* was made available by their Lordships for some forthcoming experiments, for we had worked with her before and knew that her captain and crew were always willing to give us their full co-operation. In the middle of this particular trial, however, the weather had turned sour in our normal operating area in the approaches to the Channel when, not for the first time, we had agreed mutually to transfer the remainder of it to the calmer, and infinitely more desirable, waters of the

Mediterranean. We owed much to our naval friends for putting themselves so far out on our behalf and felt the least we could do in return was to deliver the mail and newspapers to the submarine daily during her transit voyage between Portsmouth and Gibraltar. We had just completed the second drop on this particular voyage.

The submariners, for their part, were also busily engaged in making improvements to the snorkling devices which allowed submarines to travel beneath the surface of the sea whilst still running on their diesel engines, thus maintaining integrity without the tedious necessity of having to surface every so often to recharge batteries. Apparently such good progress had been made in this field that HMS *Andrew*, according to the newspapers, was even then in mid-ocean in the course of making the first trans-Atlantic crossing by a submerged submarine.

It was too good an opportunity for ASWDU to miss, for we, too, had a new piece of equipment which we were eager to try out. This gadget, our boffins maintained, should pick up and register traces of ionised gases given off by a diesel engine. Of course, if this was so, it would provide maritime aircraft with a means of localising a search for a submerged submarine whose snorkel alone was too small for radar to pick up, unless at very close range. Hence we had planned to seek out *Andrew* as she made her historic underwater crossing of the Atlantic Ocean. Whether by accident or design, information about her whereabouts was scanty, and all the naval chaps at Plymouth would tell us was that *Andrew* should have been anything between four and six hundred miles west of Ireland. However we intended to have a crack at finding her after we had delivered the goods to *Auriga*.

Geoff Bainbridge treated the Autolycus equipment like it was a child of his own making which, to a certain extent it was, for he had been working on its development since shortly after Professor Barclay had conjured up the idea. Indeed, there were those who gave Geoff the credit for having thought up its name. The code word 'Snifter' had been the original choice, but it had been considered too indicative of the equipment's function, after which Geoffrey had called upon his store of classical learning to come up with the title 'Autolycus' which, he had explained, was a 'snapper-up of unconsidered trifles'. And thus it had remained.

Bainbridge and Jock Gray, the navigator, pored over the large chart spread out on the bench, pencilling in the route most likely to have been followed by *Andrew*, and on to which Jock had superimposed wind vectors derived from his latest drift sightings.

'It could be verra guid, Geoff. The wind must be blawin' straight up her backside, and it's unco strong too. Providing there's nae ither boats aboot, your machine should get a pretty guid sniff at her!'

Bainbridge put his finger on the chart and looked at his watch.

'Thanks, Jock. How long will it take to reach this point here? Fifteen minutes, eh? Start the search pattern at eleven ten, then. In the meantime I'll go forrard and get the set warmed up.'

Geoffrey stopped by me as he passed through to his position in the nose section. As he had unplugged his earphones, I took off my headset to hear what he was saying.

'We should reach the area soon, Sir. I'm just going to get the set ready. Keep your fingers crossed!'

I could not help smiling, for Geoffrey was desperately keen to prove his pet project, the effectiveness of which, so far, had been somewhat questionable. However, all the previous tests had been made in areas where other shipping had been about, and the smoke traces from them had probably become mixed up with those of the targets we had been seeking. This was the first time we had taken Geoff's baby so far out to sea.

Jock called from the navigator's position.

'First search leg coming up, Sir. Steer three zero zero for twenty minutes.'

I set the new course on the graduated dial and pressed the button to engage the automatic pilot, when the Shackleton responded by turning gently on to the prescribed heading. The all-round visibility was good, but a choppy sea was running on top of the heavy Atlantic swell, which would make it difficult to pick out anything so small as a snorkel among the clutter of white horses. We could but hope for the best. Geoffrey's voice came through the headset.

'I think I have a trace, Sir. Maintain your present heading.'

Thus we flew towards the west in a series of zigs and zags whilst Bainbridge's device continued to register ever stronger indications as we cut back and forth across the mean course, the operator's voice rising with excitement every time the needle on the graph paper recorded another pickup. What we were doing was to fly a cone-shaped pattern by shortening the length of each leg as we neared the source of the emissions being picked up on the Autolycus. Finally he was satisfied.

'I think we've got her now, Sir. Turn on to two eight zero and carry out a radar sweep ahead.'

The other crew members had now come forward and were crowded into the flight deck, scanning ahead for the tell-tale plume of a snork cleaving the water at some fifteen knots, whilst below, in the nose section, Geoffrey could hardly contain himself.

'This is great! It's getting stronger all the time. We should see it soon ...'

Just then the radar operator reported a blip four miles ahead when, sure enough, we saw a plume of spray thrusting high in the air as the submerged submarine continued her transit across the wide expanse of ocean. Jock summed up what we were all thinking.

'Ah would'ny care to be in yon. It must be awfy stuffy doon there after fower days under the sea!'

Indeed, we airmen had much to be grateful for, although we could never get Toby Weston to agree, for he had an aversion to flying and swore he would never take off in an aeroplane. The fact that he disdained to let it worry him when his submarine let in water now and again, by putting up an umbrella to keep his uniform dry, together with a wartime award of the Distinguished Service Order, spoke volumes for the fellow's bravery but, nevertheless, he had a 'thing' about flying.

However a story, probably apocryphal, has it that, on an occasion when *Auriga* and a Sunderland flying boat of ASWDU were carrying out a sono-buoy trial from Gibraltar,

Toby had taken one of our lads for a trip in his submarine, in the course of which he had laid on a demonstration of a crash dive to such effect that they accidentally struck the bottom. Subsequently, during a few nerve-steadying drinks in the wardroom, our victim had talked the gallant Commander into coming on a reciprocal trip the following day. However, a Sunderland did not like a calm sea from which to take off and, of course, there would have to be a flat calm for Toby's first flight. When calm conditions prevailed, the technique was to taxy the flying boat at high speed in a wide circle to create waves, and to take off through them to break the adhesive effects of water against the metal hull.

On this occasion however, the captain of the Sunderland had failed to notice several large pieces of flotsam and, in the middle of his wide, high speed, taxying circle, ran into them and knocked off one of the wing floats. Naturally the trip had to be abandoned when Toby, instead of sampling the pleasure of a short flight over the Mediterranean, had to join the rest of the crew on top of a wing to help balance the aircraft whilst the captain shamefacedly taxied her ashore for the necessary repairs. From then on Toby had been more determined than ever to confine his service activities to the sea and the land.

We were pleased with the result of the Autolycus trial, which had certainly justified the Professor's faith in his invention. After all, it had been quite an achievement to home in on an object no larger than a six-foot metal pole sticking out in the middle of the Atlantic Ocean. However, we had been airborne for over nine hours so, after photographing the snork from every possible angle, decided to call it a day and head back to our base in Cornwall.

A new administrative officer had recently taken over at our base and, as he had never been up in a Shackleton, we had invited him to join us on the trip. Now that the operational job had been completed, I suggested he should sit in the right hand seat and take the controls during the long flight home. I therefore left him there, with Walker in the left hand seat to monitor the flying, whilst I went aft to stretch my legs and help Geoff prepare a fry-up for the lads. He was still bubbling with excitement.

'I can't wait to tell the Prof. What a pity he couldn't have been with us, but he got his dates all muddled up. In fact, I think things have been weighing on his mind more than he has let on, for he has become very absent minded lately. D'ye know, he offered to give me a lift in his car the other day when I got in the front passenger seat, while the Prof climbed into the back and sat there until I reminded him he was supposed to be the driver!'

Be that as it may, we were all delighted to work with him and shared Geoff's pleasure at the successful outcome of all his hard work.

It was evening before land hove in sight and we flew in to join the circuit at St Mawgan, where a strong wind was blowing from the south. This meant we could not land on the long main runway and would have to settle for the shorter one. However, we had used up most of the fuel during our twelve-hour flight and were therefore landing light. So, having taken over the controls from Walker, I invited our guest to remain where he was to watch the landing from a pilot's seat.

Although he normally assisted with such items as lowering the undercarriage and flaps during this phase, the second pilot in a Shackleton had no vital actions to perform other than to pull the four throttle levers into the fully closed position, and to hold them there, whenever the captain called 'All off'. Each pilot's position was equipped with its own throttle quadrant, below which were four levers which controlled the pitch of the propellers. I had briefed Bill about his part in the proceedings and how, as soon as I had called 'All off', he was to haul back the throttles and hold them in the fully closed position.

The runway looked very short when we turned on to finals and full flap had been put down. However, it seemed I had judged the approach fairly accurately, for we were running in to land close to the threshold and I glanced quickly to my right to make sure Bill was ready to take over the throttles as I put both hands on the control column and pulled back on it for the flare-out and landing. As soon as the boundary hedge disappeared under the nose I called Bill to close the throttles, whereupon the engines suddenly died on us and we were left to career down the runway with all four props stopped.

Fortunately there was plenty of pressure in the braking system and we were able to pull up short of the far threshold, when it was discovered that the four sets of propellers were not only motionless, but that all their blades were pointing edge-on to the slipstream. Poor old Bill, in his eagerness to do my bidding, had grabbed the wrong set of levers and, instead of clamping the throttles, had pushed the pitch controls straight through the gate and thus feathered all four engines. We would have been in the soup had it been necessary to go round again.

Maybe Toby Weston had the right idea after all!

23

JETTING INTO TROUBLE

The other diners gazed curiously at the three men occupying the corner table by the window, but it was probably the tallest of the trio who was the object of their attention, for he was completely without a hair on his head. Not that bald heads were uncommon on the Continent, but it was rare to find anyone as young and handsome as Bill so bereft of the usual thatch on top.

'I wish to goodness these people would stop staring at me. You would think they had never seen a bald head before! What's the French for "Go and take a running jump at yourselves", Sandy? I've a good mind to tell them to mind their own business!'

Bill Kent was not really upset; in fact, he was one of the most even-tempered chaps imaginable and had long since learned to expect a certain amount of curiosity from those who had not met him before, for he had lost his hair as a result of a particularly severe attack of measles at the early age of six. In any case, he would never have dreamt of creating a scene in a public restaurant, especially a foreign one at that and, besides, we were in the middle of a rattling good dinner at the time, and the wine was superb.

'Belt up, Bill. They don't mean any harm. Here, have some more wine. You might as well, for it's thrown in with the meal!'

Bill laughed as I reached for the carafe and topped up our

glasses. Jerry Roberts held his against the light to see better the dark rich bloom of the Burgundy wine.

'Yes, at least we have chosen a good place to come down. What's the name of this hotel again? Oh, Le Chapeau Rouge. I suppose that means "The Red Hat"!'

Bill, Jerry and I were stopping overnight at the hotel in Dijon, having made an emergency landing on the nearby French Air Force station at Beaune earlier that afternoon. It was still raining heavily when we finished our meal and went through to the lounge where further surreptitious glances were cast in Bill's direction by the early diners so, as it was still too wet for a gentle stroll down the street, we decided to call it a day and to turn in for an early night instead. Parting company at the top of the staircase, we each vowed to put up a silent prayer for better weather the following day, for we still had a long way to go.

I was looking forward to visiting Malta again, for I had not been there since early 1943.

*

The war having been over for nine years, things had more or less returned to normal and the pre-war squadrons of the Auxiliary Air Force, now honoured with the prefix 'Royal', had started up again and were once more making a significant contribution to the air defences of the nation. Every summer, several RAuxAF units would be sent overseas to carry out intensive training and it was customary, on these occasions, for senior members of the Staff to pay them occasional visits to check on progress. By 1953 I had completed my time in Coastal Command and had been moved back into the fighter fold in the post of Senior Air Staff Officer at the Group Headquarters responsible for air defence north of the Wash, in which a number of Royal Auxiliary Air Force squadrons operated. As the lads from the Cheshire unit were spending a fortnight training in Malta, the AOC suggested I should fly there in a Meteor jet aircraft to see for myself how the programme was coming along.

On long flights of this nature it was prudent for aircraft to fly in pairs, particularly as the single-seater Meteor Mk 8 was not fitted with any sophisticated navigational aids. Thus it was agreed that Bill Kent and Jerry Roberts would accompany me in a Meteor night fighter Mk 11, which had all the latest gubbins fitted – an arrangement which suited me admirably as the former was an ace jet pilot and Jerry a navigator of no mean ability.

We got together to plan the details of the flight.

'Right, Bill, I'll leave the navigating to Jerry and will tag on alongside, so don't get me lost! We had better leave from Tangmere, for they have Customs facilities there and it will save the bother of having to summon someone from Nottingham. All being well, we should make it with one refuelling stop at Istres.'

'That makes sense to me. Now, what do we do if one of us has to come down for any reason?'

'We'll stick together, Bill. Besides, I'll need all your expertise to get me there!'

We positioned the two aircraft at Tangmere the evening before in order to make an early start, but the Met man's forecast was not very encouraging – we could expect solid cloud cover along the entire route to the south of France, with thunderstorms likely over the Massif Mountains, he said. However, most of the route was covered by a good ground control organisation and the NF 11 was fitted with various navigational devices so, providing the cloud itself was not dense, I foresaw little difficulty in being able to keep station on the leading aeroplane, and we agreed to chance it.

After obtaining clearance from the customs officer, Bill, Jerry and I made last minute checks to make sure we had not forgotten anything: maps and courses properly marked out: radio frequency cards brought up-to-date: adaptors for the refuelling hoses and starter batteries stowed away in case we had to land at an airfield not carrying fitments for Meteors: copies of *The Air Pilot*, showing details and landing patterns for all airfields along our route: ensuring everything was firmly secured inside the aircraft. Yes, all seemed to be in order as we climbed into our aircraft and started up the engines.

We flew into cloud soon after taking off, but it was not dense and I had no difficulty keeping Bill's aircraft in sight as we climbed steadily to level off at 35,000 feet, although we were still not through the top. However, the two jet engines were behaving well and I settled down to formate on the NF 11 during the two hour flight to Istres.

It had been necessary to change radio frequencies on entering French-controlled air space and soon afterwards we ran beyond the coverage provided by the RAF Navigational G-Chain on which Jerry was relying to keep an accurate track of our position. As yet we were too far off to make voice contact with Control in the south, but it would only be a matter of ten minutes or so before we could expect to be under ground control again. Indeed, I was just thinking how easy it was all going to be, when Bill called on the radio.

'Hello One Five. My ventral tank is not feeding properly and I have only fifteen minutes fuel remaining in the main. Check yours to make sure you are all right.'

Both gauges in my aircraft were registering 'full', which indicated that the overload tank fitted beneath the belly was feeding correctly.

'Hello Two Three. I'm OK. Let me know where you intend to land in case we become separated.'

'We will try to get in at Beaune. I suspect the feed pipe has frozen up. In the meantime change over to one two one point five. Over.'

I pressed the button for the emergency frequency and listened while Bill made a *sécurité* call to alert the French control organisation. However, the wavelength was fully taken up with the voices of American pilots, none of whom seemed to be in any form of distress as far as I could gather and, as we continued to descend, Bill's voice grew ever more anxious as the precious minutes ticked away and he was still unable to get a word in edgeways. I heard him call that he only had eight minutes' fuel remaining, but the irritating chatter continued unabated.

'Mayday! Mayday! This is Rafair Two Three. Am out of fuel and require urgent controlled descent to Beaune. This is a Mayday call. Do you read?'

The effect was dramatic: The jabbering ceased immediately and the controller's voice came through loud and clear to give Bill precise instructions for the let-down and landing. By now we had our dive brakes extended and were diving steeply, turning this way and that to follow the instructions. Five thousand feet. Three thousand feet. One thousand feet, and still in cloud with heavy rain slashing against the windscreen. I dropped into line astern when I saw the undercarriage and flaps of the NF 11 being lowered. The Approach Controller had now taken over and continued to talk us down the glide path – 'You are too low – OK now. Left two degrees. Begin to throttle back. Look ahead now ...'

We broke clear of cloud at four hundred feet to see the long runway ahead, glistening through the heavy rain, when I pulled off to one side to join the circuit while Bill went straight in to land in a cloud of spray as the Meteor careered along the flooded surface.

They were standing beside their aircraft when I taxied alongside and climbed down from the cockpit.

'Whew! That was a close shave! Do you know, that wretched pipe didn't unfreeze until we were taxying in!'

By the time we had walked to the Operations Centre to thank our saviours, the weather had closed in completely and the airfield was declared unfit for any further landings. Furthermore, we also learned that Istres, too, had been similarly affected, so it was probably a blessing in disguise that Bill's fuel system had frozen up when it did. At all events, we decided to spend the night in Dijon, to the undisguised curiosity of certain French diners, as you know.

Next morning the weather was overcast, although it had stopped raining, but we were warned to look out for severe thunderstorms near the South Coast. So, once again we flew into cloud immediately after take-off, which showed no sign of breaking even when we reached our cruising altitude of 37,000 feet. In fact, I was beginning to think we would never see anything of France at all on this trip. However, we were soon in radio contact with the controller at Istres and could derive a certain measure of comfort in the knowledge that now, at least, we were under radar control from the ground.

'Hello Rafair Two Three. This is Istres Control. Thunderstorms are reported to the north of us. Do you want me to bring you in from the east or from the west? Over.'

As we were already flying through unbroken cloud, there was no way of telling where the centre of the storms lay in relation to our track and Bill could only tell him to use his own discretion. However we soon had cause to doubt the controller's choice when our surroundings grew darker and darker as we began the long let-down towards Istres. I found it necessary to fly ever closer to Bill to keep his aircraft in sight through the thickening clouds and I don't suppose we were more than ten feet apart when the full force of the storm hit us.

We were thumped this way and that, whilst huge hailstones battered relentlessly against the aircraft, creating a roar which could be heard even above the noise of the engines. Blinding flashes of lightning zigged and zagged from all angles and, on one occasion, jumped from Bill's wingtip to mine as I hung on grimly to keep him in sight. I could see from the violent movements of the NF's aelerons that Bill, too, was having to wrestle with his aircraft as he struggled to comply with the directions being passed by the Controller. Up and down, inwards and outwards, I clung to the control column with all my might to prevent it from being snatched from my grasp as the aircraft was buffeted remorselessly by the elements. At one point I swear we were thrown upside down, for the instruments had gone crazy and all my weight seemed to be on the shoulder straps as I fought desperately to keep station while we continued the nightmare descent towards Istres.

Suddenly we broke into the clear. Without warning it turned from night to day, as if we had unaccountably stumbled upon a Shangri-La. A blazing sun shone down from a cloudless sky whilst, ahead, the Mediterranean stretched into the distance like a carpet of azure blue. The runway at Istres lay to our left like a long dark blue pencil whilst, to our right, gaily coloured villas, nestling into the hills around Nice, made the scene like a picture from a fairy tale book. But behind was a solid wall of the blackest clouds I have ever seen and it was apparent we had just flown through the father and mother of all thunderstorms.

Bill and I said little as we gazed at our aircraft after taxying to the parking area; the visible damage to the machines told its own story. The nose cone of my Meteor was badly dented and every scrap of paint on the fuselage had disappeared as far back as the cockpit, whilst the leading edges of the wide air intakes had been frayed and stripped of their fabric coverings by the force of the large hailstones smashing against them. Bill's aeroplane had fared little better and we were forced to delay take-off once again while some essential patching up was carried out.

Malta still seemed a long way off!

The Met people at Istres at least gave us some encouragement for the next leg to the island, although they warned us to expect strong headwinds throughout. However, we were flying in clear weather for a change as we settled down to cruise comfortably in brilliant sunshine above the white-capped waves of the incredibly blue sea. As it is tiring to fly in close formation for any length of time, I positioned myself about a mile from the other aircraft to be able to look around and see what was going on. I reckoned that Bill, too, must have been enjoying the comparative tranquillity of the flight, for he was not keeping up his usual chatter on the radio. Thus we flew on, over the southern tip of Sardinia, heading towards Malta.

It was some time before I noticed the other aircraft's wings rocking back and forth and, on flying closer to find out what was wrong, saw Bill making vigorous hand signals to me. At first I thought he was merely making a few rude gestures as he stuck two fingers in the air and pointed to his earphones, but soon realised he wanted me to change from the number one radio set to the number two.

'Hello One Five. My number one set is on the blink. You will have to take the lead. Call Luqa on one one four point seven. You should be able to raise them in about ten minutes. Watch your fuel though, for Jerry reckons the wind is blowing at over seventy knots up here.'

It was now late afternoon, with the sun at our backs, and the forward visibility was at least one hundred miles. Indeed, it was not long before Malta came into sight far off in the distance but, with such a strong wind to battle against, it was still much too early to start letting down. In fact, it was slowing us down so much that it was going to be touch and go whether we would have enough fuel to get there, for a glance at the gauges showed there was little more than enough for another twenty minutes in the air. A call to Bill confirmed he was in the same predicament.

'No, One Five, I am not going to make Malta. Jerry has worked out a course for Tunis which will take us fifteen minutes. Steer one six five, and I suggest we shut down one engine during the descent.'

I had already decided to do this, for we could save a considerable amount of fuel this way and were not going to lose much speed while going downhill. And so we made yet another unscheduled stop where we had to use our combined linguistic knowledge of French and Italian to make ourselves understood sufficiently to talk the Tunisian authorities into refuelling the two aircraft, thanking our lucky stars we had brought with us the special adaptors.

It was dark when we finally landed at Luqa and careered along the brightly lit runway to be met by a somewhat disgruntled squadron commander who had been hanging about all day awaiting our arrival. But what a relief it was to be there at all!

*

Several of the Auxiliaries had arranged for their wives to join them while their squadron was undergoing its intensive training period on the island, so it was not a case of all work and no play. Now a happy group was sunning itself on the rocks at St Paul's Bay after a delightful swim in the warm waters of the Mediterranean and tucking in to the contents of a picnic basket thoughtfully provided by one of the ladies. There was much laughter and bantering as we recounted the string of misfortunes which had befallen us during the flight out from England, doubtless embellished to suit the occasion. However I noticed, every now and again, one of the girls casting surreptitious glances in the direction of Bill's shiny pate. Bill also noticed her interest.

'Yes, my dear, it must have been a terrifying journey. I had a full head of hair before we set off to come here!'